I LOVE GOD'S SENSE OF HUMOR;
I Just Wish He'd Let Me in on the Joke

Stan Toler

BEACON HILL PRESS
OF KANSAS CITY

Copyright 2006
by Stan Toler and Beacon Hill Press of Kansas City

ISBN 978-0-8341-2249-9

Printed in the
United States of America

Cover Design: Keith Alexander

Library of Congress Cataloging-in-Publication Data

Toler, Stan.
    I love God's sense of humor : I just wish He'd let me in on the joke
 / Stan Toler.
    p. cm.
    Includes biblical references.
    ISBW 0-8341-2249-9 (pb<.)
    1. Christian Life—Biblical teaching.   I. Title
 BS680.C47T65 2006
 248.4—dc22

   2006000142

20 19 18 17 16 15 14 13 12

Contents

Dedication

To Kent Hubbard, a brother beloved. Thanks for making my life easier each day. Your work of excellence as Pastor of Congregational Ministries at Trinity Church of the Nazarene has enabled me to write books, conduct seminars, and travel the world.

Acknowledgments

I express my special thanks to Jerry Brecheisen, Deloris Leonard, Pat Diamond, Bonnie Perry, Barry Russell, and the entire Beacon Hill Press team for their assistance with this book.

About the Author

Stan Toler is founder of the Vibrant Group, an agency focused on training leaders to reach optimal effectiveness in their various disciplines, and is senior pastor of Trinity Church of the Nazarene in Oklahoma City. For several years he taught seminars for John Maxwell's INJOY Group, a Christian leadership development institute. He currently serves as executive director of the Toler Leadership Center, located on the Oklahoma City campus of Mid-America Christian University. Toler has written more than 50 books, including his best-sellers *God Has Never Failed Me, but He's Sure Scared Me to Death a Few Times; The Buzzards Are Circling, but God's Not Finished with Me Yet; God's Never Late, He's Seldom Early, He's Always Right on Time;* his popular "Minute Motivators" series; and his latest book, *The Secret Blend.*

For information on seminars, to schedule speaking engagements, or to contact the author—

Stan Toler

P.O. Box 892170

Oklahoma City, OK 73189-2170

stoler1107@aol.com

www.stantoler.com

Introduction

Have you ever felt as though you were the only one in the crowd who didn't get a joke? It's embarrassing and frustrating. The joke-teller obviously had a great sense of humor. His or her delivery was impeccable, the timing was perfect, and the topic was relevant. But you just didn't get the punch line. It flew over your head like a bat in the barn.

Life's a lot like that. It's supposed to have its giggles along with its gasps. Yet sometimes the giggles seem to fly over our heads. Just ask some of the great characters of the Bible: Moses, Joshua, David, Daniel, Joseph, and many others. They struggled with finding the humor in some horrifying situations. Yet they still mustered up enough courage and faith to overcome the obstacles in their life.

The late Johnny Carson, arguably the king of television talk shows and one of the most spontaneously funny entertainers of all time, was known for his opening monologues. Always relevant, Johnny could take a topic from the daily news and turn it into a hilarious commentary.

He was also as well known for his *recovery* as he was for his *delivery*. Sometimes his audience didn't get one of his jokes. They missed the point entirely, leaving the studio with dead air space and only a few faint chuckles. Carson excelled in recovering the moment. He would stare into the camera, pull the boom mic down, and pretend he was announcing a "blue light special" in an aisle of a discount store—or he would repeat the punch line with a slow, condescending tone. The audience loved it, and they usually responded with more laughter than if they had gotten the joke the first time.

This book is about life's awkward moments. It's about the silence that fills the air after trouble, tragedy, struggle, or stumbling. It's in the same genre as that of some of my previous books: *God Has Never Failed Me, but He's Sure Scared Me to Death a Few Times! God's Never Late; He's Seldom Early; He's Always Right on Time,* and *The Buzzards Are Circling, but God's Not Finished with Me Yet.* This book will help you deal with some of the most pressing problems in your life—with a smile on your face.

As a matter of fact, God *does* have a sense of humor. How do I know? For one thing, the Bible says so. Ps. 2:4 reads, "The One enthroned in heaven laughs." For another, He made kangaroos, zebras, and anteaters! But throughout history, His people didn't always get the joke. He was opening oceans wide enough for enemy chariots and then pulling the plug, making axe heads float, pulling coins out of the mouth of fish, turning fig trees into instant firewood, and so forth. All the while, some of His people often stood watching with blank stares and empty hearts. Even Christ's disciples had to have interpreters for some of His monologues.

But each of the incidents or stories had a lesson that went further than first seen. One didn't necessarily need a killer sense of humor to get the punch line. He or she just needed a great sense of faith—an ability to see that God could get a person to Jerusalem even if He took him or her through Cleveland to get there.

It's also about recovery. *Overcoming* is the theme. In these pages you'll learn how to overcome—

- Obstacles
- Disappointment
- Temptation

- Anger
- Fear
- Inadequacy
- Doubt
- Hopelessness
- Failure
- Loneliness

Each chapter will put a familiar face to these challenges—biblical faces. Because God's Word is eternally relevant, the solutions of history are just as important today as they will be until the end of time. You will see that God has already spoken to the problems of your life, in a real-life situation recorded in His Word.

There aren't any daytime talk show quick fixes here. I can promise you only a spiritual workout. (No pain, no gain!) I can also promise you that there will be some smiles along with the seriousness, and grins along with the gains. Bible folk didn't spend all their time in church (whether it was the Tabernacle, the Temple, the synagogue, or a house church). They lived and walked with others. They put their faith to the test "uptown," as well as "down country."

Their struggles were as human and as real as any you will see on a network news report. They formed their faith in the heat of the day and let it solidify in the cool shadows of midnight. They met God on the playing field, not just in the locker room. Their victories were accompanied by bruises.

It's my prayer that you'll find some key principles in these pages. I've discovered them on my own spiritual journey. As I followed the lives of the biblical giants in writing this book, I discovered a common theme: God's faithfulness. He not only has a purpose for our lives—He has power to go along with it. Some obstacles are too tall for me, but God is taller.

Don't Be Afraid to Take Baby Steps

Overcoming Obstacles

Some things aren't worth the trouble. Others are. And going to a college football game is one of them. It wasn't a dark and stormy night, like the setting in one of Snoopy's unfinished novels in the *Peanuts* comics series. It was a cold and rainy afternoon in Norman, Oklahoma. The University of Oklahoma was playing another unworthy opponent, and I was there to make sure the opponent knew how unworthy they were.

Was I alone in the misery of the cold and rain that accompanied that fall football outing? No. Did that make it any more comfortable? No again. Eighty-some thousand souls had joined me for the occasion. Thankfully, for once in my ministry I didn't have to provide the refreshments! I don't remember how much I paid for the ticket. It was either too much, or someone had given it to me. I just remember what I went through to see another lopsided win by the Big 12 champions.

It started with the parking lot. Too full. Too far away. The reserved section of the Gaylord Family-Oklahoma Memorial Stadium parking lot was neatly laid out, newly striped, and within a few paces of the entrance. It was reserved for the major donors, the faculty, the university president's mother-in-law, and the family of a recruit that was still digesting a T-bone steak as he walked those baby steps to the gate.

I wasn't in the reserved section. If memory serves me right, I think I was in a nearby state—either Texas or Arkansas. Not being a major donor, an adjunct professor, or a recruit, I found myself in one of the parking lots next to the university's power plant, a mile or so from the gate. No newly painted markings graced this parking lot, just an oil leak from an old Ford pickup truck parked next to my car, a truck normally used to haul fertilizer to lawns and shrubs around the campus.

Dressed loyally in my crimson and cream, I made my way to the stadium. What seemed like hours later, I reached my goal: the refreshment stand. Football games are best observed with a huge container of popcorn, a jumbo hotdog, and a 24-ounce cup of diet soda. But by the time I got there, the friendly alumni folks were out of them all! So I rushed to the section marked on my ticket, and there, in the spirit of the occasion, I stood for the rest of the game. I did my best to watch my team play as an endless throng walked in and out of my row to get to the refreshment stand—or someplace else.

OBSTACLES ARE JUST PART OF THE PROCESS.

It's the same in life as it is in going to football games. You don't always get the reserved section. The sun isn't always shining. Sometimes it rains. And sometimes people get in your way.

Ask Naaman. He was a commander in the king's army. The Bible calls him a "great man." In 2 Kings 5:1 we read, "Naaman was commander of the army of the king of Aram. He was a great man in the sight of his master and highly regarded, because through him the LORD had given victory to Aram." He must have had medals pinned to his uniform. His brand-new chariot probably had chrome spinner wheels and a 10-CD stereo, with a woofer that would scare the staunchest of horses.

Then the kicker. One description trumped the others: "He was a valiant soldier, but he had leprosy" (v. 1). The best and the worst were linked together in the same résumé. It may look like yours. The "bests" and the "worsts" may be different. But the dilemma is the same. You had it all going for you, but suddenly the bad news arrived. The obstacles rumbled in, and life was never the same again.

"Is this some kind of joke, Lord?" you ask either out loud or under your breath. "If it is, I guess I just don't get it." You've probably arm-wrestled with God, just as Naaman did at the first notice of the white spots on his arm—spots what would soon grow to eat away his skin, that would reduce his life's status from "great" to groveling. I love the way the Lord took Naaman from the pinnacle to the pits—and back. It's a great story and full of help for those of us who are the victims of what seems to be one of life's "practical jokes."

NAAMAN WASN'T EXEMPT FROM LIFE'S CALAMITIES

Naaman had everything going for him, including membership in the human race. And that membership would ultimately spell trouble for him. He was born into a family tree that had bad roots and weak bark. He was one of Adam's kin. You remember Adam, don't you? The first man. The first farmer. The first husband. The first to disobey God—and the first to suffer the consequences. We read in Gen. 2:7-9,

> The LORD God formed the man from the dust of the ground and breathed into his nostrils the breath of life, and the man became a living being. Now the LORD God had planted a garden in the east, in Eden; and there he put the man he had formed. And the LORD God made all kinds of trees grow out of the ground—trees that were pleasing to the eye and good for food. In the middle of the garden were the tree of life and the tree of the knowledge of good and evil.

Adam had it all going for him, and then he lost it all by doing the one thing God asked him not to do: eating from the tree of the knowledge of good and evil.

Did I mention that Adam wasn't alone in the Garden of Eden? God had given him a wife—to make sure he did everything right: Naaman's great-great-great-great-great-great-great grandmother, Eve. But she didn't do everything right. She made a fruit bowl, and Adam got bowled over! He got food poisoning—and passed it along to all generations after him. You can read the whole sordid story in Gen. 2—3. They both disobeyed God and suffered the consequences that entered the blood stream of humanity and ended up as spots on Naaman's skin.

> Sin entered the world through one man, and death through sin, and in this way death came to all men. . . . Death reigned from the time of Adam to the time of Moses, even over those who did not sin by breaking a command, as did Adam, who was a pattern of the one to come (*Rom. 5:12, 14*).

For Adam, life's obstacles come from his *obstinate* attitude! He refused to obey God, and life took a turn for the worse. Obstacles come even when we don't sin. It's just part of life. Thank you very much, Adam! But like a man in the Old Testament who went from being a commander to being a catastrophe, we can overcome them. Let's learn from him.

Naaman's privilege couldn't prevent the problem. He may have been one of the richest men in the neighborhood, but the poorest man there wouldn't trade places with him. He had leprosy.

The disease didn't fit Naaman's lifestyle. He was a cut above the crowd. But now he had a very base problem.

Obstacles don't care about lifestyles. They come and go, no matter how much you have in your 401(K). Problems don't bow to people. *People bow to problems.* It's as natural as corn-on-the-cob at a church picnic.

Naaman's position couldn't prevent the problem. Naaman was a "commander," one promotion away from sitting on the throne of Israel. He was at the height of his military career. But just when he thought he had it all under control, he lost control. Life threw him a sucker punch in the form of a terminal illness. Some of the greatest military or political leaders of history have been defeated not by human enemies but by common illnesses. It's like the nursery rhyme:

> *Humpty Dumpty sat on a wall;*
> *Humpty Dumpty had a great fall.*
> *All the king's horses and all the king's men*
> *Couldn't put Humpty together again.*

When obstacles come, your position on the corporate ladder doesn't make you taller than they are. Naaman's position couldn't prevent the problem.

Naaman's plans couldn't prevent the problem. Just to show you how the king's commander is so much like all of us, we see that he tried to circumvent the calamity with a human plan.

> Now bands from Aram had gone out and had taken captive a young girl from Israel, and she served Naaman's wife. She said to her mistress, "If only my master would see the prophet who is in Samaria! He would cure him of his leprosy." Naaman went to his master and told him what the girl from Israel had said. "By all means, go," the king of Aram replied. "I will send a letter to the king of Israel." So Naaman left, taking with him ten talents of silver, six thousand shekels of gold and ten sets of clothing. The letter that he took to the king of Israel read: "With this letter I am sending my servant Naaman to you so that you may cure him of his leprosy" (*2 Kings 5:2-6*).

I love God's sense of humor. He sits on the throne of the heavens, with all power and might and wisdom, and watches us humans use straw swords to fight against the things that threaten us.

Posturing—"I will send a letter to the king of Israel."

Bartering—"Naaman left, taking with him ten talents of silver, six thousand shekels of gold and ten sets of clothing."

"There has to be a way out of this predicament!" we say. "Let's see—if I do this or that, maybe . . ." Naaman knew the drill: bring gifts. Pay your own way. But money can't buy healing. Human schemes and plans may make us feel comfortable for the moment, but they don't work in the end. Life's downturns or dangers are usually immune to human designs. You and I must have a higher, more powerful, source for deliverance.

No matter where Naaman went and what he took with him, he still had a problem: leprosy. It was a human calamity without a human cure. But Naaman took a right turn at the intersection of his life.

NAAMAN'S CALAMITY CALLED FOR AN UNCOMMON CURE

Obviously "All the king's horses and all the king's men couldn't put Humpty together again." When the king of Israel got the letter, he had, as they say in my home state of West Virginia, a "hissie fit."

As soon as the king of Israel read the letter, he tore his robes and said, "Am I God? Can I kill and bring back to life? Why does this fellow send someone to me to be cured of his leprosy? See how he is trying to pick a quarrel with me!" (v. 7).

The king thought Naaman was trying to make him look bad. He knew he didn't have the power to heal Naaman's problem. In spite of the letter. In spite of the gold. In spite of the brand-new wardrobe.

Watch the sequence.

God took over when humanity gave up. Uncommon cures for the obstacles of our life begin with trusting God instead of self. That's just as important for our salvation as it is for our healing.

You see, at just the right time, when we were still powerless, Christ died for the ungodly. Very rarely will anyone die for a righteous man, though for a good man someone might possibly dare to die. But God demonstrates his own love for us in this: While we were still sinners, Christ died for us (*Rom. 5:6-8*).

Just when we thought we had enough spiritual funds to make bail, to get out of the prison of our past or future, God took over. God supplied an uncommon source of deliverance— His only Son. The Judge paid our penalty with His own life!

Naaman discovered an uncommon cure for his calamity.

When Elisha the man of God heard that the king of Israel had torn his robes, he sent him this message: "Why have you torn your robes? Have the man come to me and he will know that there is a prophet in Israel" (*2 Kings 5:8*).

God didn't glance at His caller ID and say, "It's Naaman! Will he never learn how to deal with his obstacles?" No, the God of compassion and mercy simply and patiently sent an ambassador: Elisha, the prophet.

Elisha, the poor prophet. Poor enough at one point to live off biscuits baked by a widowed mom. Human enough at one point to sit under a tree and weep over his failures. But rich enough in faith to approach the commander of the king's army with a solution for his leprosy: *God*.

How we have it mixed up at times! "When all else fails, try God." Instead, we ought to simply say, "Try God. Give up pouting, pining, and planning! Give it over to God."

Naaman started toward the cure when he started toward God. God is a perfect gentleman. He won't barge into our plans. He won't interrupt us in the midst of our tantrums and tears. He won't start removing our obstacles without our permission. "So Naaman went with his horses and chariots and stopped at the door of Elisha's house" (v. 9).

Even when I don't get the joke, I love God's sense of humor. I'm out here on the highways and byways of life searching desperately for a cure for my calamities, and God looks through the window of heaven and wave—as I drive by!

Every fiber of His holy being longs to cry out, "Won't you stop in?" But He just waits, patiently, for travelers like you and me to stop at "Elisha's house"—the place of surrender, the place of healing.

Naaman stopped the healing process when he tried to regain control.

Elisha sent a messenger to say to him, "Go, wash yourself seven times in the Jordan, and your flesh will be restored and you will be cleansed." But Naaman went away angry and said, "I thought that he would surely come out to me and stand and call on the name of the LORD his God, wave his hand over the spot and cure me of my leprosy" (*2 Kings 5:10-11*).

Naaman was willing to go on the *Dr. Phil* show, but he wasn't willing to listen for his advice. Or, as Julie Andrews suggested so eloquently in another era, he wasn't willing to take the "spoonful of sugar" to "make the medicine go down."

The man in need of an uncommon cure for his common calamity put the cure on "pause." How? By trying to set the rules, by telling God what should be done instead of listening for God to tell him what to do. "I thought that he would surely come out to *me.*" He illustrated our own tendency to question God.

Namaan tried to save himself. He thought his way was better than God's, his plan more powerful than God's: "'Are not Abana and Pharpar, the rivers of Damascus, better than any of the waters of Israel? Couldn't I wash in them and be cleansed?' So he turned and went off in a rage" (v. 12).

Now before we get all puffed up like a lemon meringue pie topping, let's think about our own journey. Have there not been times when we've tried our own shortcuts? Haven't we tried to insert our Plan B into God's Master Plan?

"I know it's a big obstacle, Lord. But let me suggest that instead of . . . we might try. . . ."

Then the voice of heaven rings in our ears through the words of another prophet, Isaiah: "My thoughts are not your thoughts, neither are your ways my ways" (Isa. 55:8).

WHEN NAAMAN OBEYED GOD, THE OBSTACLE WAS OVERCOME

God's prophet Elisha didn't promise healing in the river Naaman chose. The healing was in the river *God* chose. It was as different as the Mississippi River and the Atlantic Ocean! God didn't meet Naaman's need until Naaman obeyed God's plan. Common obstacles are overcome with uncommon obedience.

Everything in us says, "There has to be a better way." But God knows the best way. That's what the Wisdom Writer was trying to tell us: "There is a way that seems right to a man, but in the end it leads to death" (Prov. 14:12).

Naaman listened to the right voice. See what happened next:

Naaman's servants went to him and said, "My father, if the prophet had told you to do some great thing, would you not have done it? How much more, then, when he tells you, 'Wash and be cleansed'!" (*2 Kings 5:13*).

When we take our obstacles into our own hands, we have a tendency to listen for big voices: booming TV commercials, brazen advertisements, big, expensive promises.

Naaman didn't get what he wanted—and needed—until he got off his high horse and listened to his footmen, his servants. It's the small voice that whispers to our hearts that's more important than the big voice that appeals to our heads. Elijah, Elisha the prophet's mentor, learned that lesson hiding in a cave in fear of the obstacles in his own life.

He went into a cave and spent the night. And the word of the LORD came to him: "What are you doing here, Elijah?" He replied, "I have been very zealous for the LORD God Almighty. The Israelites have rejected your covenant, broken down your altars, and put your prophets to death with the sword. I am the only one left, and now they are trying to kill me too."

The LORD said, "Go out and stand on the mountain in the presence of the LORD, for the LORD is about to pass by." Then a great and powerful wind tore the mountains apart and shattered the rocks before the LORD, but the LORD was not in the wind. After the wind there was an earthquake, but the LORD was not in the earthquake. After the earthquake came a fire, but the LORD was not in the fire. And after the fire came a gentle whisper (*1 Kings 19:9-12*).

It was the "gentle whisper" that caught Elijah's attention. He was moved to abandon the cave of fear and get back on the job, not by a loud display of God's power but by a gentle voice of His presence. Similarly, Naaman began the healing process—again—by *stopping* and *stooping* to hear the tiniest message from God's messengers.

Naaman did the right thing. "So he went down and dipped himself in the Jordan seven times, as the man of God had told him" (2 Kings 5:14). Everything about the process was seemingly out of a commander's character:

Listening to lowly servants.

Washing in strange rivers.

Following the instructions of a prophet instead of a political leader.

But it was the right thing to do. It was God's way. It was the way to wholeness. And no matter how senseless it looked on the outside, inside Naaman knew there was healing at the end of the road. God's "detour" didn't have a "No Outlet" sign at the end. When Naaman simply said "Yes" to God's Holy Spirit, his own spirit began to be made whole.

Naaman saw the right results. "And his flesh was restored and became clean like that of a young boy" (v. 14).

Upon learning that he was diabetic, legendary Nazarene evangelist Uncle Bud Robinson was said to have remarked, "I asked God to make me sweet, and he overdid it!" That's Naaman language. God didn't just heal Naaman's leprosy—He did an "extreme makeover." Naaman's "flesh was restored and became clean like that of a young boy" (2 Kings 5:14).

NAAMAN'S CALAMITIES TURNED INTO A CONFESSION

The saying goes, "The best advertisement is word of mouth." It's the same in the Kingdom. When God does something for us—when He removes obstacles—the best thing to do is sing His praises. Every crisis in life is a challenge to our faith. But when God helps us meet the challenge, we ought to give Him the credit.

Naaman displayed his gratitude by praising God. "Then Naaman and all his attendants went back to the man of God. He stood before him and said, 'Now I know that there is no God in all the world except in Israel'" (v. 15). The Bible says that God inhabits the praises of His people. Gratitude is a place where God dwells. When you do what God asks you to do, He'll do it—one way or another. Then, when He does what He promised to do, the parental advice to a child who has just received a blessing comes into focus: "What do you say?" Anything less than "Thank you" is unacceptable.

Naaman displayed his humanity by bartering with God.
"Please accept now a gift from your servant," he said (v. 15).
God understands our humanity. He became one of us in the
person of His Son, the Lord Jesus Christ. If Jesus was tempted
to turn stone into bread, the enemy can surely tempt us to
turn bread into stone—to lessen the miracle, to think we
played a greater part in the process than we really did.

Naaman tried to give God his credit card instead of a
thank-you note. Instead of simply acknowledging that there
was no other way out of the obstacle than God's way, Naaman's humanity began to show like a gorilla at a garden show.

The prophet answered, "As surely as the LORD lives,
whom I serve, I will not accept a thing." And even though
Naaman urged him, he refused. "If you will not," said
Naaman, "please let me, your servant, be given as much
earth as a pair of mules can carry, for your servant will never again make burnt offerings and sacrifices to any other
god but the LORD" (*2 Kings 5:16-17*).

There he goes again! Trying to set the rules, trying to tell
God's messenger how to do the whole worship thing. But Elisha knew God wanted a heart of praise more than a piece of
land. He wanted a heart of obedience more than an offering in
the plate, even more than perfect attendance at church.

Obstacles once overcome are stepping stones—not mile-
stones. God doesn't bring us "here" to leave us here. He
brings us "here" to take us *there.*

Naaman took his miracle with him. "'Go in peace,' Elisha
said" (v. 19). So Naaman went on.

Converted to Christ at a Billy Graham crusade, a Holly-
wood actor by the name of Stuart Hamblen put his praise for

what the Lord had done in his life into the lyrics of an immortal gospel song, "It Is No Secret." Naaman continued his journey with the blessing of the Lord on him, a blessing he had received on knees of obedience. Others sought that blessing (v. 20), because Naaman couldn't keep his mouth shut about how God had used muddy water to make him totally clean.

Hold on Tightly,
but Go Lightly
Overcoming Disappointments

Residents of the southern United States would probably call 2004 "the year of the hurricane." Charley, Frances, Ivan, and Jeanne came ashore like all-pro linebackers in the NFL, leaving the coastal land bruised and battered like an opposing tackle who had missed training camp. Millions were evacuated, only to return to find lifelong dreams scattered in piles of rubble. Television news reporters caught the anguished faces of disappointed people searching through the debris to find whatever was left of their possessions. Our hearts were touched by the reports of those whose lives would never be the same.

They're not the first to return home to ruin and rubble. Travel back to Bible times. After 70 years in exile, the children of Israel returned to the city of Jerusalem, only to discover that the magnificent Temple built by King Solomon had been destroyed by the Babylonians. The Temple was not only their house of worship; it was their gathering place, their learning center, their symbol of God's covenant with them. There the high priest entered the Holy of Holies to talk with Jehovah on their behalf. There the sounds of their rejoicing in song and instrument echoed off the marbled walls. There the tithes and offerings of gold or grain were brought to the storehouse as a reminder of God's abundant blessings. There animal sacrifices were made in anticipation of the day when their Messiah-Savior would bear the sins of the whole world.

Disappointment hung in the air over the debris like ugly drapery. In their hearts, the Israelites had lost everything dear to them. Jerusalem's Temple lay in ruins. And they didn't even have the heart to rebuild. Reconstruction was slower than a stalled snail. The taunts of the enemy kept the contractors indoors. And the apathy of the believers kept the scaffolds on the ground for 18 long years. Finally the Lord said, "Back to work!"

"On the twenty-first day of the seventh month, the word of the LORD came through the prophet Haggai" (Hag. 2:1). In so many words, the prophet would say, "Get over it. I know you're living in the valley of disappointment. But there's a Temple to be built. God needs a meeting place, and so do His people. The sun's going to shine again—and you're going to be religious reflectors!"

Haggai's Old Testament prophecy is like a road map for those of us who wander in the deserts of our own disappointments. It's as relevant as driving directions on a global positioning satellite receiver. Let's look at some important principles for dealing with those disappointments.

DISAPPOINTMENTS ARE HOPES THAT NEED REMODELING

The dictionary suggests that our disappointments are actually hopes that don't meet our expectations. It's like shooting a triple bogey on a par 3 hole in golf. The hope you had on the tee isn't the same when you're in the sand trap next to the green—and you left your pitching wedge at the last hole!

When they returned to Jerusalem, the children of Israel had a different vision of the Temple than when they had left. The Lord said through Haggai,

> Speak to Zerubbabel son of Shealtiel, governor of Judah, to Joshua son of Jehozadak, the high priest, and to the remnant of the people. Ask them, "Who of you is left who saw this house in its former glory? How does it look to you now? Does it not seem to you like nothing?" (*Hag. 2:2-3*).

"Does it seem like nothing?" That's one of those *Double Jeopardy* television game show questions—which already have answers. *Of course* it seemed like nothing! Everyone from the governor to the high priest could see that! Everything that was once beautiful about the Temple was only a faded memory now. The majestic walls were in ruins. The courtyard was torn up. It was a mess—just like some of the situations in our lives. Disappointment is as common as a telephone call during dinner—annoying and often depressing, but expected now and then. Yet disappointments are moments of opportunity—once we see where they come from.

Disappointments are ruined appointments. "God loves you and has a wonderful plan for your life." Maybe you've heard that heartwarming introduction to the gospel. God does have a wonderful plan for each of us. But part of that wonderful plan is to allow some dandelions in our otherwise beautiful yard. The apostle Paul wasn't a stranger to ruined appointments. On one of his great New Testament missionary tours, he had plans to go to a city called Thessalonica. He wrote a letter to Christians there, telling of his changed appointment:

> Brothers, when we were torn away from you for a short time (in person, not in thought), out of our intense longing we made every effort to see you. For we wanted to come to you—certainly I, Paul, did, again and again—but Satan stopped us (*1 Thess. 2:17-18*).

Satan had ruined his appointment and had turned it into a disappointment.

As long as you're going to take a journey of faith, you might as well realize that the enemy of your faith will do everything possible to try to get you bumped from the flight! He'll use anything (and anyone) possible to bring detours of disappointment to your travel plans. That's his job!

Disappointments are changed appointments. God has the last word in our appointments—and disappointments. He uses them for our spiritual well-being. For example, I've sat in many airports waiting for flights and have heard the dreaded announcement over the intercom telling waiting passengers that the flight was overbooked. With one of those trained smiles, the airline employee at the ticket counter suggests options: One, give up your seat and fly anywhere, compliments of the airline—the following day, of course! Two, make a reservation for the next available flight. Neither option made me feel like singing the "Hallelujah Chorus." But as a frequent flier across the nation and around the globe, I've come to terms with such changes of schedule.

The irritation lasts only for a while. The solution is still on the calendar. So far, I've returned home to Oklahoma City 100 percent of the time. And besides, the changed appointment may have been for my welfare. We all know of those instances when a change in travel plans has resulted in someone missing a deadly crash. So the disappointment may have been for my good! If nothing else, it gave me time to pray, to read, to get acquainted with fellow passengers, and to work on developing my level of tolerance.

Let's face it: our travel itinerary was established before the stars were born. "The steps of a good man are ordered by the LORD: and he delighteth in his way" (Ps. 37:23, KJV). *Steps* or *stops*: if we'll honestly see our disappointments as divinely changed appointments, it will be easier for us to "take the next available flight."

Our disappointments are simply times when we can work on reconstructing our hopes. They're building times. They don't always make earthly sense—but they make sense in heaven! Look again at Haggai's prophecy.

Disappointments are training times. "'Be strong, all you people of the land', declares the LORD, 'and work. For I am with you,' declares the LORD Almighty" (Hag. 2:4). In other words, work out your disappointments. We know what "workout" means—it means work! It means having an overall plan to use extreme effort that will result in an "extreme makeover."

In a spiritual sense, our "workout" includes a Personal Trainer. "Work," the Lord said. "For I am with you." We're never really alone in our disappointments. The God who went to both the manger and the Cross will obviously go *anywhere* with us—even through the deserts of our life, through our disappointments. During the disappointing times, His promises are *clearer*. During the disappointing times, His strength seems even *greater*. During the disappointing times, His love seems even *dearer*.

He is there, personally watching over our "strength training." Just as a weight lifter has a spotter standing by, who's ready to lift the weights off in case they're too heavy, our Personal Trainer has promised that no weight will be more than we can handle (1 Cor. 10:13).

OUR PERSONAL PROMISE

We live in an interesting age of technology. We have electronic gizmos that can even put live television on pause—so we can go to the kitchen for another diet soft drink and an apple turnover. But God's Word is *never* on pause during our problems. Our disappointments are divine opportunities for God to roll out His covenant. God in Christ has promised to take us to the finish line. Phil. 1:6 says, "Being confident of this, that he who began a good work in you will carry it on to completion until the day of Christ Jesus."

Israel recognized that promise *on their way to captivity in Babylon*, and *on their return to Jerusalem*. "This is what I covenanted with you when you came out of Egypt. And my Spirit remains among you. Do not fear" (Hag. 2:5). Both directions were marked with God's promises. Wherever you are on the journey, there's a promise along the path. Don't be afraid of the schedule changes. God's flights are never overbooked!

OUR PERSONAL PERSPECTIVE

At a special Thanksgiving service in Lancaster, Ohio, I heard E. Stanley Jones say, "When the heart is right, thanksgiving is natural." We don't have much choice in our looks. We're subject to pairs of designer genes that have been passed down through the family. But we do have a choice in how we look at things—even how we look at disappointments. We can actually see them as a *plus*. How?

1. *Use the disappointment to cultivate a grateful heart.* As bad as the disappointment is, it could be greater. Just look around. Compared to some other folks' disappointment, ours may seem like winning the Publishers Clearing House sweepstakes.

2. *Use the disappointment to development a confident mind.* God's power is at work even in this problem. We didn't see it coming, but *He* did! And when He saw it coming, He immediately had a plan for our survival.

3. *Use the disappointment to strengthen purpose.* We started working on "purpose" as little children. Give us a "can't," and in our hearts it became a "will." We can turn that negative trait into a positive. "I *will* get through this. I *will* trust God for deliverance. I *will* see the strengthening process. The psalmist showed purpose: "I will remember the deeds of the LORD; yes, I will remember your miracles of long ago. I will meditate on all your works and consider all your mighty deeds" (Ps. 77:11-12).

DISAPPOINTMENTS ARE PREPARATION TIMES

"Timing is everything," one well-known comedian explained of his success. But those of us who have faced sudden disappointments immediately wonder what timing has to do with success. At some inappropriate time, our plans crumble. Our dreams shatter. Our schedule is horribly interrupted.

It was the same for the people of Israel. Their long-standing traditions, their "life as we know it," their worship in the Temple of Jerusalem were suddenly interrupted by a kidnapping and a terrorist attack. But the prophet Haggai reminded them that they weren't living in an earthly time zone—they were on "EST" (*God's eternally supernatural time*).

This is what the LORD Almighty says: "In a little while I will once more shake the heavens and the earth, the sea and the dry land. I will shake all nations, and the desired of all nations will come, and I will fill this house with glory," says the LORD Almighty (*Hag. 2:6-7*).

DISAPPOINTMENTS ARE PRELUDES TO GOD'S POWER

I hate to say it, but I've been in some worship services in which the prelude by the church organist was so bad that neighborhood dogs were howling! Thankfully, when the congregation began singing, it drowned out the dischords and missed chords of the lady who must have spent all her organ lesson money on garage sales.

The prelude was awful for the Israelites too. At first glance everything was out of tune: in captivity away from their homes, serving the enemy in a foreign country, and returning to rubble and ruin.

It's not unlike some of our own trips. We left when we didn't want to, we headed in a direction we didn't want to go, and when we returned, nothing was the same. But somehow in the process, everything turned out for the better. Why? God was using our problem as a prelude for revealing His power.

"In a little while," God said through the prophet. In other

words, "Relax. We're right on schedule—my schedule. I'm simply preparing you for the best, which is to come!" Sometimes we have to go through the problematic preparation times in order to get to the "power zone." We see it all around us.

In nature, the rose understands that there will be a preparation time of being out of sight, buried in the cold earth, sprinkled with acidic powder, and subject to the elements. Yet in its very being it knows that one day the blooming will come. The disappointing preparation time will reveal a color, texture, and beauty that will make gardeners gasp.

Likewise in cooking, West Virginia biscuits must have some clue that they're in for some rough times—some beating, kneading, thinning, shaping, and baking—before they'll be fit for display on a Southern breakfast table and a baptism with redeye gravy! The preparation time leads to the perfection.

DISAPPOINTMENTS ARE OPPORTUNITIES FOR GOD'S POWER

Haggai spoke God's words: "I will shake all nations" (Hag. 2:7). Israel's disappointments were opportunities for divine intervention. Let me illustrate. My sons aren't like me simply in appearance. They're like me in experience too. They've been through some of the same scrapes I've been through. In different ways, in a different climate, but the scrapes were similar. We share bruised knees. We share a couple of bad grades in school. We share some glares and stares, punches and crunches by neighborhood bullies. And we also share an intervention by dear ol' Dad!

More than once my father stepped into the middle of a neighborhood "disagreement." He had been there all the time. His strength was just as strong. His justice was right. And he was just as loving. But I didn't need to rely on those characteristics 'til the bully with the closed fist started promising me a "trip to the moon"!

When the opportunity came, my dad took over. He stepped in between the bully and the bullied. His words instantly settled the argument. His strength became my strength. It's the same with our Heavenly Father. His character or characteristics never change. As He says in Mal. 3:6, "I the LORD do not change. So you, O descendants of Jacob, are not destroyed." And He is *always* present in our problems and disappointments. Sometimes I don't get the joke. Sometimes I don't understand why He seems to "stand on the shoreline" for a while before wading into my troubled waters. But His timing is perfect. He uses the *opportunity* to make known His *ability*. I put my emotional transmission into "P"—Panic, not Park—and He suddenly takes over. Stepping in between the bully and bullied, he settles the argument with His Word. His strength becomes my courage. Paul put it right: "As the Scripture says, 'Anyone who trusts in him will never be put to shame'" (Rom. 10:11).

DISAPPOINTMENTS ARE PROMISE TIMES

God said through the prophet, "In this place I will grant peace" (Hag. 2:9).

"This is a good place to plant a promise," God was seemingly saying through the prophet. I've found that to be true in my own life. For example, when I was in college, I made a monetary pledge during a missionary conference. It was money I didn't really have at the time. It was money I didn't even *expect* to have. But it was money that God told me to give, so I gave it. And God gave it back—with interest! I have to confess that at the time I was a bit disappointed that God would ask me to give what seemed like a partial payment on the national debt (in comparison to my income). But all the while, He was planning to put one of His promises in motion: "Give, and it will be given to you. A good measure, pressed down, shaken together and running over, will be poured into your lap" (Luke 6:38).

Now, I wasn't disappointed to be in a position to obey God. I was just disappointed that I had so little to give Him. He knew that. And He also knew that He had me covered! My little 'ol gift wouldn't make the Treasurer of heaven the slightest bit nervous.

Haggai found that out. The Holy Spirit spoke to his heart, "'The silver is mine and the gold is mine,' declares the LORD Almighty. 'The glory of this present house will be greater than the glory of the former house,' says the LORD Almighty" (Hag. 2:8-9). Not only would the children of Israel have a big enough "credit line" to rebuild the Jerusalem Temple—they would also have some money in their savings accounts! Disappointment times are promise times!

DISAPPOINTMENTS REVEAL GOD'S EXTRAVAGANCE.

From gold to grace to grit, God has promised enough of what we'll need to recover from our ruin and rubble. Read these words from Paul: "He said to me, 'My grace is sufficient for you, for my power is made perfect in weakness.' Therefore I will boast all the more gladly about my weaknesses, so that Christ's power may rest on me" (2 Cor. 12:9). I was 11 years old when my father was killed in a work-related accident. As I wept about the loss and was preparing to tell my younger brothers about the accident, God wrote me a check in the form of a promise: "The LORD is my shepherd, I shall not want" (Ps. 23:1). His extravagant promise was big enough for my excruciating situation.

It will be the same in your life. You may be suffering the number-one setback in your entire life. None could compare to this one. Life has played its worst practical joke on you—and you don't get it. But the Great Shepherd has a promise in the bank: You "shall not want." You'll get through this, not on your resources but on His. His salvation is perfect for your setback.

DISAPPOINTMENTS REVEAL OUR FINAL VICTORY

Haggai shared God's secret in 2:7. Who? "The desired of all nations," the Messiah Savior. What? "Will come"—He will make an appearance to fulfill His promise. Where? "This house" —when and where you need it most. In other words, salvation is on the way! "For his anger lasts only a moment, but his favor lasts a lifetime; weeping may remain for a night, but rejoicing comes in the morning" (Ps. 30:5).

All the bullies of time are no match for the "blessed appearing of our Lord and Savior Jesus Christ." All the disappointments and problems of this age are no match for God's final and all-consuming appearance.

He won't "turn the other cheek" then. He'll be swinging a worthy sword of justice. Right will reign, and wrong will be slain. Health will win over sickness. Prosperity will win over poverty. Life will win over death.

So forge ahead with faith. Reach for your restoration. Let God turn your disappointments into an exciting dynamic. If He can light a fire under a nation and cause its citizens to get back to work to rebuild a fallen Temple in Jerusalem, He can light your fire—and cause you to get back on track, even if you wandered off the road and crashed in a ditch.

You can overcome your disappointments.

Jump In—Even If You Don't Know How to Swim

Overcoming Fear

Humorist Dave Barry wrote, "All of us are born with a set of instinctive fears—of falling, of the dark, of lobsters, of falling on lobsters in the dark, or speaking before a Rotary Club, and of the words 'Some Assembly Required.'"[1] I don't know about the being "born with," but I do know that for those of us fortunate enough to be alive, fear is as common as orange barrels on a summer highway. The dictionary suggests that "fear" comes from a Greek word that means "to attempt." It is further defined as "an unpleasant, often strong emotion caused by anticipation or awareness of danger."[2] The outer limits of fear—extreme fear—turn to phobia, an emotional bondage to something or someone.

Old Testament character Joshua could have been a poster child for fear; but instead, he was known for being an *over-comer*. Born into slavery, he rose to become an assistant to the great leader Moses. When Moses died, Joshua inherited the "whole nine yards." He became the leader of the children of Israel, winning their wars and leading them to the Promised Land. Along the way, he carved out a trail of faith and courage that any one of us could follow. From the battle for Jericho, to dividing the land of Israel, to the twelve tribes without a civil war, to the crossing of the Jordan, to his last will and testament, Joshua's attitudes and actions placed him in the "top seed" on heaven's team.

His commissioning is one of the standout sections of God's Word (Josh. 1:1-18). It would be good for us to take a closer look, since God's commands and Joshua's responses are exactly the things we need to know if we are going to overcome fear in our own lives. At least four basic fears are addressed in the opening chapter of Joshua.

FEAR OF THE UNKNOWN

God called Joshua to take His people on a trip to the unknown—without Mapquest!

After the death of Moses the servant of the LORD, the LORD said to Joshua son of Nun, Moses' aide: "Moses my servant is dead. Now then, you and all these people, get ready to cross the Jordan River into the land I am about to give to them—to the Israelites. I will give you every place where you set your foot, as I promised Moses. Your territory will extend from the desert to Lebanon, and from the great river, the Euphrates—all the Hittite country—to the Great Sea on the west. No one will be able to stand up against you all the days of your life. As I was with Moses, so I will be with you; I will never leave you nor forsake you" (*Josh. 1:1-5*).

Franklin D. Roosevelt said, "The only thing we have to fear is fear itself." If the 32nd president of the United States had made his speech on the first day of Israel's journey, it would have sounded like a stand-up comedian's routine. They were probably thinking about a list of fears rather than a philosophy of fear: unknown enemy soldiers, wild beasts, hunger, thirst, exposure to the elements, and so on. This looked to be the mother of all trips!

You've probably faced such a trip. Perhaps it wasn't a trip across the Judean wilderness. It may have been (or may be) a trip across town to your new home, or across the hallway to your new office, or across the state to a medical clinic. The unknown can be a little scary. The Book of Joshua gives us some guiding principles.

First, remember what God promised. "I will give you every place where you set your foot, as I promised Moses" (v. 3). God promised abundant supply. The children of Israel may not have known what lay ahead, but God did. This was familiar territory to Him. In fact, every rock and every ridge were born in His heart before the first sunrise. He would be their supply line, as well as their strength. His promises would hold them, even when everyone else had broken theirs. Every step would be a step forward, even when they had to take a bypass. Every day would be a day closer to the sunset, even when the sun didn't shine.

One credit card company claims you shouldn't leave home without their card. But most credit cards have a limit. God's promises are *unlimited*. The psalmist David gave us his testimonial:

> I have not departed from your laws, for you yourself have taught me. How sweet are your words to my taste,

sweeter than honey to my mouth! I gain understanding from your precepts; therefore I hate every wrong path. Your word is a lamp to my feet and a light for my path (*Ps. 119:102-105*).

I don't know where your journey may take you. You may have some painful detours. You may get a couple of pebbles in your shoe. The sun may hide behind a few clouds. There may be some steep hills to climb, some wide valleys to cross, some high floodwaters to flee. But you still don't have to be afraid. God has given you a promise for every inch, every step, every mile. Your journey is well known to Him. That's why He filled His Word with road signs!

Second, remember what God promised to do. "No one will be able to stand up against you all the days of your life" (Josh. 1:5). God promised to be a Big Brother to the Israelites. They seldom went anywhere without the threat of attack hanging around them, like the cloud of dust around the "Pigpen" character in Charles Schultz's *Peanuts* comics. They were the children of promise. And the children *without promise* were always intent on taking theirs away. But they couldn't. Humanity's devices can't break God's promises. "All the days of your life" is a "fur piece," as they say down South.

Yet the fear of the unknown prompts us to be in a state of heightened alert. Security is a billion-dollar business in these post-9/11 days. And almost every event has its "security force." A recent convention of *Star Wars* fans even had their security personnel dressed as Galactic Empire "storm troopers" to blend in with the crowd. Security products abound, from computer firewalls to armored vehicles to bulletproof designer suits; the fear of unknown terrorists stalking the streets or cyber-landscapes of our society has produced a huge windfall to the security experts.

A first-century philosopher named Syrus characterized the mind-set of many people who live in the 21st—"What we fear comes to pass more speedily than what we hope." You don't have to be in their number! Let me say it again: Your unknowns are well known to God. "Those who hope in the LORD will renew their strength. They will soar on wings like eagles; they will run and not grow weary, they will walk and not be faint" (Isa. 40:31). Don't forget who's in charge of security: God.

Third, remember what God promised to be. "As I was with Moses, so I will be with you; I will never leave you nor forsake you" (Josh. 1:5). God promised to be Joshua's best friend. (That's being in better hands than Allstate!) There would be times when the young leader would have to make some lonely decisions. There would be times when he would have to stand alone, holding the commands of God in front of a stubborn people. But on the day of his commissioning, God whispered to his heart, "Joshua, you'll never be alone. I'll be with you." What was the extent of that promise?—"As I was with Moses, so I will be with you." Joshua had some "size 12" shoes to fill; but he also had a mighty big Friend to help him fill them!

I once heard Billy Graham at one of his crusades say, "The greatest fear comes when God is a stranger." God doesn't want to be a stranger to you. He wants to be your dearest friend. In fact, He made the first move. "The angel said to them, 'Do not be afraid. I bring you good news of great joy that will be for all the people. Today in the town of David a Savior has been born to you; he is Christ the Lord'" (Luke 2:10-11). God knocked on the door of your heart—in person! The promises of the Old Testament would be forever fulfilled in the person of God's only Son—"A man of many companions may come to ruin, but there is a friend who sticks closer than a brother" (Prov. 18:24).

You'll never go anywhere He has not already been; and you'll never go there alone. Overcoming the fear of the unknown starts with knowing who's traveling with you. In every circumstance of your life, remember that God always has your best interests in mind. He will never let you down.

FEAR OF FAILURE

A Chinese proverb says, "Failure is not falling down—it is refusing to get up." But no matter how you slice the philosophical pie, failing most often makes you feel as if you got the smallest piece—as if you're a failure! It does something else: It makes you afraid to try again. God warned Joshua not to "turn from it to the right or to the left" (Josh. 1:7)—but to stay on track:

> Be strong and courageous, because you will lead these people to inherit the land I swore to their forefathers to give them. Be strong and very courageous. Be careful to obey all the law my servant Moses gave you; do not turn from it to the right or to the left, that you may be successful wherever you go. Do not let this Book of the Law depart from your mouth; meditate on it day and night, so that you may be careful to do everything written in it. Then you will be prosperous and successful. Have I not commanded you? Be strong and courageous. Do not be terrified; do not be discouraged, for the LORD your God will be with you wherever you go (*Josh. 1:6-9*).

How would he stay on track? What steps would he take

to keep from tripping over the starting line and falling flat on his face like an Olympic runner with Super Glue on his or her track shoes? We had better look carefully. We have some starting lines to face of our own.

First, join the obedience group. "Be careful to obey all the law my servant Moses gave you" (v. 7). "My servant" caught Joshua's attention. Of course, he had witnessed the personal and corporate success of his mentor firsthand. Moses had set the bar pretty high, far enough for God to call him a "servant"—a personal assistant to the Creator of the universe! You've heard the expression "Good work if you can get it." Well, Joshua got it! He skipped all the middle rungs on the corporate ladder by choosing to follow the leader.

Whether you're shopping in Saks or Sears, you'll have people all around you whose lives have been affected positively or negatively by the choices they've made. We all come to the crossroads of decision—spiritual or otherwise. And what we decide will influence both our direction and our destination.

You may be handcuffed to the fear of making a decision (maybe because of a wrong decision you made during the last go-round). Let me give you the key. Choose the *right* thing. Once you do what's right, I can assure you that you won't have to worry about the decision any longer. The psalmist said, "The fear of the LORD is the beginning of wisdom; all who follow his precepts have good understanding. To him belongs eternal praise" (Ps. 111:10).

I can almost hear you from here. "Whoa, Nelly! You're telling me to overcome fear by *fearing*? You're telling me to fear the Lord?" That's right. "Fear" in the context of the Scripture verse is not being "afraid" of something; it's being "in awe." In this case, it's the wisdom of God. Fear, or be in awe of, God's totally unique ability to give you the supernatural sense to choose right.

Join the "obeying" group. It may look like the "slow group" at first. But at second glance, you'll find it to be the most contented, the most courageous, and the most committed. Those who have chosen to obey God's law are those who have discovered the inner peace that brings a smile even in the midst of a storm.

Second, read the owner's manual. "Do not let this Book of the Law depart from your mouth; meditate on it day and night, so that you may be careful to do everything written in it" (Josh. 1:8). God called Joshua to a 10-gallon task. He wasn't going to give him teacup resources! He gave him the instructions—the owner's manual, the Scriptures. Look at the heavenly postscript at the end of verse 8: "Then you will be prosperous and successful." Joshua didn't have to live in fear over giving the right orders. He simply followed *God's* orders. They were right in the first place.

If you've ever spent Christmas Eve putting a toy together without reading the instructions, you know what ignoring them may lead to—in the best-case scenario, a toy that doesn't function properly. You'll have to fill in your own blanks for the worst-case!

For example, after you've put the handlebars on backwards, the chain on the wrong sprocket, the kickstand upside down, and the seat facing the wrong way, you'll probably come to the conclusion that the best way to put a bicycle together is by reading the owner's manual first. It will save you high anxiety, and it will make your child's Christmas morning a whole lot safer!

It's the same in life. Fear of failure is overcome by following the instructions of God's Word.

Pray

Rest

Give

Love

Forgive

Serve

God made it simple for us. He even gave someone the insight to put the instructions in chapter-verse form. Sixty-six separate books in one Bible—a whole library of resources to help us overcome the things that have a tendency to overwhelm us!

Third, live by the "buddy system." "Do not be terrified; do not be discouraged, for the LORD your God will be with you wherever you go" (v. 9). You can be sure that more than once Joshua reached for the unseen hand. Whether it was in the heat of a battle or the middle of a committee meeting with the 12 tribes of Israel, Joshua took God at His Word. God's hand was only a prayer away. It didn't tremble in the battle. It wasn't influenced by the intimidation of the "experts." Joshua could walk across the busy streets of his life with his hand in the hand of his greatest friend and helper—God.

You may not be crossing streets. You may be treading hostile waters. Who knows? You might even be swimming with a few sharks. But know this: the one whose hand you choose to hold not only *builds* sharks—He walks on water! Up or down, you're a winner!

Live by the "buddy system." Choose to get a good grip on courage by getting a good grasp on God. And as long as we're thinking about it, you might as well know that God's grip is better than yours! "So do not fear, for I am with you; do not be dismayed, for I am your God. I will strengthen you and help you; I will uphold you with my righteous right hand" (Isa. 41:10).

Interestingly, there are those who are just as afraid of success as they are of failure.

FEAR OF SUCCESS

"So Joshua ordered the officers of the people: 'Go through the camp and tell the people, "Get your supplies ready. Three days from now you will cross the Jordan here to go in and take possession of the land the LORD your God is giving you for your own'" (Joshua 1:10-11).

I don't know what Joshua was thinking at that moment. But if he was like some folks I know, he might have been thinking, "Fine, and what do I do when I get there?" There was as much unknown about Joshua's *claims* as about his *calamities*, his future as much as his present. Would there be questions he couldn't answer? Would that level of success make him airsick? Who knows? The only thing Joshua knew for sure is that the Promised Land would make him just as dependent on the promises of God as the wilderness.

I recently heard of a lottery instant-millionaire winner whose wife divorced him. Another was arrested for driving under the influence of alcohol and served jail time. Another went bankrupt. It looked as if they couldn't handle money or success. They're not alone. I've met some people who have spent most of their life on the first rung of the corporate ladder because they were afraid of heights. Let's just say they were level-headed to a fault!

You may be there with them. You may be as fearful of success as you are of failure. God's word to Joshua provides some remedies.

First, inventory your supplies. "Go through the camp and tell the people, 'Get your supplies ready'" (v. 11). God wasn't going to let Joshua climb without a backpack. He had given the leader and his followers all they needed for the trip: supplies. Now all they needed to do was check their list.

Barbecue sauce.

Sunscreen.

Hiking boots.

Swiss Army knife.

It was all there. God had packed their survival kits for them, even before the journey.

Are you facing success like a mouse in a cheese factory? Do you see the goal but don't know if you have the strength to get there? Inventory your supplies. God has equipped you for this mountaintop. He wouldn't bring you this far without making sure you have a flag to put on the top! And He wouldn't start you on the journey without giving you your own backpack. Inventory what He has given you the ability to do—and then do it, for heaven's sake.

Second, work your plan. "Three days from now you will cross the Jordan" (v. 11). Joshua had the goal in mind. Now he simply needed to take the steps toward the goal, not necessarily *giant* steps—just steps. God promised the *place*; Joshua needed to set the *pace*. Three days. One day at a time.

The goal line may be in sight. But your fear of success may be keeping you from making the first step. Remember—it takes only one. One plus one plus one equal one. That's not great math, but it's a good way to get a head start on your getting ahead: One *ambition* plus one *decision* plus one *action* equal one *realization*.

Third, make a start. God said, "Cross the Jordan here to go in and take possession of the land" (v. 11). Joshua's possession of the Promised Land began where he was, not 30 miles from the spot where he received the instructions. Where he was: *this side* of the Promised Land.

At one time Bill Gates had to learn how to use a computer. Serena Williams swung at her first tennis ball. Dorothy Hamill laced up her first pair of skates. Pavarotti sang his first note. Peyton Manning threw his first pass. Bill and Gloria Gaither wrote their first song. Casting Crowns made a demo CD. The greatness of the greats had a beginning. And so will you.

Will it make you perspire? Probably. Great tenor Luciano Pavarotti was quoted as saying, "Am I afraid of high notes? Of course I am afraid. What sane man is not?"[3] You may be afraid of high notes, but that doesn't mean God won't help you reach them. You'll simply have to sing first. You'll have to make a start.

An additional fear puts a fence around the rest. Change is more than parking meter feed. It's a challenge you'll face at every level of your climb to the top.

FEAR OF CHANGE

To the Reubenites, the Gadites and the half-tribe of Manasseh, Joshua said, "Remember the command that Moses the servant of the LORD gave you: 'The LORD your God is giving you rest and has granted you this land.' Your wives, your children and your livestock may stay in the land that Moses gave you east of the Jordan, but all your fighting men, fully armed, must cross over ahead of your brothers. You are to help your brothers until the Lord gives them rest, as he has done for you, and until they too have taken possession of the land that the Lord your God is giving them. After that, you may go back and occupy your own land, which Moses the servant of the Lord gave you east of the Jordan toward the sunrise" (*Josh. 1:12-15*).

I'm sure all the "fighting men" of Reuben, Gad, and Manasseh's tribes were suddenly so far out of their comfort zone that they couldn't have seen it with a Hubble space telescope. They were to go *before* their brothers into battle. (Think arrows!) This wasn't the usual strategy. Up until now they had marched as an army. Now they were marching as a unit. "We've never done it this way before" might well have crossed their minds.

Is God trying to deliver you from "cementitis?" Has he brought a new opportunity into your life and scared the life out of you in the process? Sudden change. A new route. Fallen fences in your "comfort zone." There's good news: God will help you face change; you don't have to be afraid. Here's how:

Focus on the plan. "Remember the command that Moses the servant of the Lord gave you" (v. 13). Joshua was reminded that he wasn't flying by the seat of his pants. This journey had a road map. Every new bend in the road, every new mountain, every new battle was covered. The great leader had only to take the steps; God would take care of the rest. He was watching over them like an eagle. "His eyes are on the ways of men; he sees their every step" (Job 34:21). Joshua and the boys would be in a new territory, but they wouldn't be in an uncharted place. God had mapped the journey—including the battles.

"This road doesn't look familiar to me," you might say. It may not. You may be faced with a brand-new route, and you're beginning to get the shakes. Calm down. Relax. God's looking over you. Work the plan. The plan from the beginning was for you to put your trust in the Lord. To tie your weakness to His strength. To cash checks from His wisdom account. To accept payments from His eternal inheritance.

Focus on your purpose. "You are to help your brothers" (v. 14). Joshua had a clear goal in mind. "Help your brothers." Take this route. Work as a unit instead of an army. Divide, and you will conquer.

The *territory* may be new to you, but you have the same *target.* What you've determined in your heart that you should do—or be—is always on the front burner. Keep your eye on the goal line. You may have to do a few zigzags, like a roller skater with six wheels, but you'll still make it around the rink before closing time. Does the change of plans still hyperlink to our purpose? Then go for it! "We know that in all things God works for the good of those who love him, who have been called according to his purpose" (Rom. 8:28).

Henry Wadsworth Longfellow once said, "What are fears but voices airy? Whispering harm where harm is not." You probably couldn't have lit Joshua's light with that phrase—at the beginning. His first listen to the command of God probably brought him a little intimidation. His mentor was dead. The people would have to trust his secondhand experience. The journey would be tough and the enemy mean. But Joshua trusted God. And as a result, the people who followed him trusted God as well.

I like their commitment:

Then they answered Joshua, "Whatever you have commanded us we will do, and wherever you send us we will
go. Just as we fully obeyed Moses, so we will obey you.
Only may the LORD your God be with you as he was with
Moses. Whoever rebels against your word and does not
obey your words, whatever you may command them, will
be put to death. Only be strong and courageous!" (*Joshua
1:16-18*).

This is the kind of commitment that will help us face the
uncertainties of our day.

1. I am committed in my mind. "Whatever you have
   commanded us we will do."

2. I am committed in my heart. "We will obey."

3. I am committed in my strength. "Be strong and
   courageous."

Fear of the known—or the unknown—begins with a commitment to put a trembling hand into the hand that doesn't
shake in the winds of time. It rests in the eternally reliable
plans and power of an unfailing God. You may be as nervous
as the parents of a newborn baby in a room full of relatives
with head colds, but you can make it. You can conquer the
greatest fears with a strong faith—and survive!

Stand for Something, or You'll Fall for Anything

Overcoming Temptation

Temptation wouldn't be so bad if it didn't make you want to do things you shouldn't do! Fact is, we live in a temptation-driven society. From television commercials to song lyrics to billboard ads, somebody's continually trying to get us to push the edge of decency, security, or spirituality. Whether it's a "reality" show or a "dramatic series," television broadcasting doesn't seem to be complete without scantily clad actors, dim lights, saxophone music, and actors in houses or rooms where they don't belong.

Pay-per-view is even worse. No one has to drive down an alley and park in a nearby lot anymore. The person just clicks a button on the remote, and the local cable company will take him or her to a porn shop on the airwaves. The problem is, the "pay-per-view" turns into a "view-per-pay"! Paul writes, "The one who sows to please his sinful nature, from that nature will reap destruction; the one who sows to please the Spirit, from the Spirit will reap eternal life" (Gal. 6:8).

Our society is being affected by a "Desperate Housewives" mentality. For the price of a selfish moment, we're making payments on wrecked homes, shattered hearts, and broken spiritual vows. In one sense, the WYSIWYG (what you see is what you get) computer term is becoming a reality in millions of lives. What is seen with the eyes funnels to the mind, which in turn ends up in the heart. No wonder the psalmist made a pledge to God: "I will set before my eyes no vile thing. The deeds of faithless men I hate; they will not cling to me" (Ps. 101:3).

So what's new these days? Only the technology. But temptation isn't a current affairs phenomena—it's a historical problem, reaching all the way to the Garden of Eden. The first woman, Eve, offered to fix a fruit salad for her husband, Adam. It wasn't a matter of bad food preparation—it was a matter of the wrong ingredients. And the result wasn't indigestion—it was insubordination. The horrible scenario is referred to as "the fall."

Now the serpent was more crafty than any of the wild animals the LORD God had made. He said to the woman, "Did God really say, 'You must not eat from any tree in the garden'?" The woman said to the serpent, "We may eat fruit from the trees in the garden, but God did say, 'You must not eat fruit from the tree that is in the middle of the garden, and you must not touch it, or you will die.'" "You will not surely die," the serpent said to the woman. "For God knows that when you eat of it your eyes will be opened, and you will be like God, knowing good and evil." When the woman saw that the fruit of the tree was good for food and pleasing to the eye, and also desirable for gaining wisdom, she took some and ate it. She also gave some to her husband, who was with her, and he ate it (*Gen. 3:1-6*).

THE PROBLEM OF TEMPTATION

God placed His creation in a perfect setting. Everything they needed was supplied by heaven. There was only one restriction: Adam and Eve were not to eat from the tree of the knowledge of good and evil—the tree of calamity. But the temptation was too great. Notice several things about the incident:

- *First, an evil force was behind it.* "The serpent was more crafty" (v. 1). Satan, in the form of a snake, was the instigator of the problem. It wasn't a frontal assault. It was a thought of doubt and disobedience planted in the mind: "You will not surely die" (v. 4). (That's probably why snakes aren't allowed to talk out loud anymore!)

- *Second, the motive was self-pleasing, not God-pleasing.* "You will be like God, knowing good and evil" (v. 5). The enemy of their faith even used the good for his wicked purposes. Eve wanted to taste what it was like to live on the other side of Eden—God's side. But she didn't want to be like Him in character, only in power.

- *Third, the temptation started in the senses.* "When the woman saw . . ." (v. 6). God created us to react to taste, touch, sight, sound, and smell. That was for both our preservation and procreation. Satan used those God-given attributes to cause Adam and Eve to tumble like a president down the last step of an airplane exit ramp (as in the infamous incident involving former president Gerald Ford of the United States).

- *Fourth, giving in to the temptation affected those around her.* "She also gave some to her husband, who was with her, and he ate it" (v. 6). This may have been the first case of "fruit flies." Eve ate the forbidden fruit, Adam took a taste, and they "flew" out of fellowship with God. Disobedience against God's Word always results in a bad trip!

THE REALITY OF TEMPTATION

Another fact of temptation is that it includes a wide circle of friends. Temptation isn't a solo gig. The apostle Paul said, "No temptation has seized you except what is common to man" (1 Cor. 10:13). How common? "Then Jesus was led by the Spirit into the desert to be tempted by the devil" (Matt. 4:1). Jesus himself was in the circle of the tempted. If hell's troops would dare to take on the very Son of God, they certainly won't be afraid to march around your campsite! Think of it! The Creator of the universe had to take a personal stand against the suggestions of Satan.

Temptation is like sweat bees at a Sunday School picnic: predictable, disheartening, disruptive, and sending people in all directions. It's *predictable* in that it will surely come into your life. It's *disheartening* because it catches even the most careful Christian off guard. It's *disruptive* in the way that it diverts attention, ruins focus, and, as I've said before, indirectly affects the lives of those around us. The fact that it *sends people in all directions* is particularly interesting.

There's a wide range of reaction to temptation. In Jesus' case, the outcome was determined by who He was. "We do not have a high priest who is unable to sympathize with our weaknesses, but we have one who has been tempted in every way, just as we are—yet was without sin" (Heb. 4:15). "Without sin!" Jesus never surrendered to the sly suggestions of Satan. His final words to the enemy at His temptation in the wilderness: "Away from me, Satan! For it is written: 'Worship the Lord your

God, and serve him only'" (Matt. 4:10). Seeing the enemy's response is like watching your favorite sports team whip the tar out of its opponent: "Then the devil left him, and angels came and attended him" (v. 11). The temptation episode ended with a victory party—and the angels brought the refreshments.

Others haven't been so victorious.

Peter, one of Jesus' disciples, had his own temptation episode. Up until the trial of Jesus, the disciple had been as faithful as the geyser in Yellowstone National Park (Mark 14:27-30). But the temptation to blend in with the crowd, rather than taking a stand for Christ, put him in the most awkward position of his discipleship.

> While Peter was below in the courtyard, one of the servant girls of the high priest came by. When she saw Peter warming himself, she looked closely at him. "You also were with that Nazarene, Jesus," she said. But he denied it. "I don't know or understand what you're talking about," he said, and went out into the entryway. When the servant girl saw him there, she said again to those standing around, "This fellow is one of them." Again he denied it. After a little while, those standing near said to Peter, "Surely you are one of them, for you are a Galilean." He began to call down curses on himself, and he swore to them, "I don't know this man you're talking about." Immediately the rooster crowed the second time. Then Peter remembered the word Jesus had spoken to him: "Before the rooster crows twice you will disown me three times." And he broke down and wept (*Mark 14:66-72*).

I think it took the apostle by surprise. He was heading toward the Disciples Hall of Fame, and all of a sudden the devil tempted him to take the "Jesus First" bumper sticker off his chariot. Sadly, it only took a few words from a peasant girl and a couple of smirks from some folks at the marshmallow roast outside the courtroom where Jesus was on trial for the batteries in Peter's loyalty to run low. *Peter the devoted* gave in to temptation and became *Peter the deceived*.

At first glance, we could conclude that he was hanging around the wrong campfire. True, but the problem goes even deeper. Peter made a personal decision about his temptation—a decision that goes all the way back to square one. He was born with a choice to either obey or disobey God. It's called "free will." Only a gracious and mighty God could offer such a selection to humans. It's seen in His invitation to the Israelites: "This day I call heaven and earth as witnesses against you that I have set before you life and death, blessings and curses. Now choose life, so that you and your children may live" (Deut. 30:19).

"Choose life!" You can almost hear the voice of God echo across the hills and valleys of time. It's as if He were saying, "Choose the *delights* of obedience over the *dangers* of disobedience!" Peter had an inner choice between Column A and Column B on the menu—and he chose from the wrong column. He was born with the possibility of a wrong choice, but he didn't have to make it.

THE PURPOSE OF TEMPTATION

You might ask, "I don't get the joke! Why would God come up with this temptation thing in the first place?" The answer: He didn't. He knew all about it—from the beginning of the beginnings—but He didn't invent it to set traps for His trusted ones. Temptation came from another source.

"When tempted, no one should say, 'God is tempting me.' For God cannot be tempted by evil, nor does he tempt anyone; but each one is tempted when, by his own evil desire, he is dragged away and enticed" (James 1:13-14). I'm not trying to play theological dodge ball here; I'm just saying conclusively that *temptation* comes from the *tempter*. If you look at the forensics of every crime against God, you'll find the DNA of disobedience—and the source of that disobedience is the same as in the Garden of Eden.

Leave it to the Almighty to turn the negative into a positive, however. He can use temptation for our spiritual strength training. James the apostle suggests that we can even face temptation with a spiritual smile on our faces:

> Consider it pure joy, my brothers, whenever you face trials of many kinds, because you know that the testing of your faith develops perseverance. Perseverance must finish its work so that you may be mature and complete, not lacking anything (*James 1:2-4*).

It worked for Joseph (Gen. 39:1-10). The man who would become an official in Egypt started out as a shepherd. In between, he faced and overcame temptation. His life teaches us about overcoming the spiritual pest that crawls around everyone's attic or basement: temptation.

THE TIMING OF TEMPTATION

As I've said, God's Word is a "global positioning system." It not only tells us where we are but also shows us how to get to where we're going. So if your destination is heaven, you ought to be thankful that God himself has given you a route through the wilderness. Learn from Joseph's journey.

1. Temptation comes when you least expect it.

Like a scene out of the old television series *Bonanza*, Joseph and his brothers were herding stock, in this case sheep. But there were as many "flies in the ointment" as there were flies on the sheep. Joseph wasn't exactly the favored brother. He was the baby of the family. His brothers were insanely jealous. So they cooked up a pot of revenge and made Joseph the main ingredient.

Now Joseph had been taken down to Egypt. Potiphar, an Egyptian who was one of Pharaoh's officials, the captain of the guard, bought him from the Ishmaelites who had taken him there. The Lord was with Joseph and he prospered, and he lived in the house of his Egyptian master. When his master saw that the Lord was with him and that the Lord gave him success in everything he did, Joseph found favor in his eyes and became his attendant (*Gen. 39:1-4*).

Suddenly Joseph wasn't on the ranch anymore. He was a slave in the royal household. As you'll see later, God turned the journey into a victory. But it was a startling first step. In one moment he was the favored son, but in the next he was a bondservant. His testing came suddenly—as if often does. Temptation doesn't send warning signals as does The Weather Channel. You may be going along at the speed of life when all of a sudden you hit a speed bump that would knock the wheels off a HUMMER.

2. Temptation comes when you're least able to resist it.

Temptation often comes after a great success. Joseph was in a place of prominence; but in that place he would face a great testing. Prominence brings its own set of problems. Prominent people have fallen from pulpits, corporate offices, or thrones—right after a great achievement. The altitude often makes one light in the head!

The election is over, and you're the new president of the Humane Society.

You've just had the biggest Friend Day attendance in the history of Sunday School.

Your new worship center is so big you could store an airplane in it.

Your job promotion puts you in charge of the department where you once handled the mail.

Your new house makes the other houses in the neighborhood look like U-Haul trailers.

Crash!

It's true even in football. For example, catch a team relaxing with a big lead, and they're likely to let up on the defense. Just when they're ready to throw a celebration and pour Kool-Aid all over the coach, the opposing team senses a weakness and makes its move. Coach Paul warns, "If you think you are standing firm, be careful that you don't fall!" (1 Cor. 10:12).

Temptation also may come after a great loss. You're spiritually and emotionally vulnerable. You're too tired or sick to maintain your spiritual equilibrium.

The one you love just said, "I don't love you anymore."

The job that was promised to you is given to the boss's nephew.

You took a risk in the stock market, and now the "bears" are meeting you for lunch—and you're the entrée.

Crash!

The devil is a master of timing. He knows that "right" moment to make "wrong" an easy choice. He's an unseen "professional wrestler" who waits to pin you to the mat. "Our struggle is not against flesh and blood, but against the rulers, against the authorities, against the powers of this dark world and against the spiritual forces of evil in the heavenly realms" (Eph. 6:12).

Does he have to win every match? Of course not! You can overcome his best moves. Joseph did, and so can you. Read on to see how.

THE STRENGTH TO OVERCOME TEMPTATION

Joseph's greatest temptation came after he was promoted to authority in Egypt:

Potiphar put him in charge of his household, and he entrusted to his care everything he owned. From the time he put him in charge of his household and of all that he owned, the LORD blessed the household of the Egyptian because of Joseph. The blessing of the LORD was on everything Potiphar had, both in the house and in the field. So he left in Joseph's care everything he had; with Joseph in charge, he did not concern himself with anything except the food he ate. Now Joseph was well-built and handsome, and after a while his master's wife took notice of Joseph and said, "Come to bed with me!" (*Gen. 39:4-7*).

Money, lust, and power. Joseph had the opportunity to live a life that some would only fantasize about. But Joseph had a higher calling. God had placed him in the palace as a representative of heaven. He couldn't afford to be a captive to earth's agenda. Satan is a great liar. He would make us believe

that: (a) we're the only ones who face temptation, (b) temptation can't be overcome, and (c) even if it could, we don't have
strength enough to be an "overcomer." Joseph's life teaches
otherwise, giving us some steps in overcoming temptation.

1. Reclaim your right to say "No!" Joseph said "No!" to
the boss's wife: "But he refused. 'With me in charge,' he told
her, 'my master does not concern himself with anything in the
house; everything he owns he has entrusted to my care" (v.
8). The greatest privilege Joseph had was that of guarding his
character. He insisted on keeping his word—to God, to himself, and to his earthly master.

Maybe you've said, "Yes," when you knew in your heart
that it was the wrong answer. Reclaim that right. You don't
have to hit the rewind button on your life. You don't have
to go down that road again. You have a personal right to *do
what's right.* One of the great incidents in Scripture is when
Joshua gathers his family around him in the midst of a disobe-
dient nation and makes a personal choice, for himself and for
his family:

> If serving the LORD seems undesirable to you, then
> choose for yourselves this day whom you will serve,
> whether the gods your forefathers served beyond the
> River, or the gods of the Amorites, in whose land you are
> living. But as for me and my household, we will serve the
> LORD (*Josh. 24:15*).

That personal decision affected an entire nation.

Your choice may not have such national or international
influence. But you must know that it will still have an influence
—on others and in your own life. Character is catching! Joseph
would be forever known by his refusal to disobey God's law.
"No" is not a popular word in this self-indulgent world. But

"No" is still a word that can make a difference between a life of regret and a life of rejoicing.

2. Repent of any known sin. Joseph explained further, "No one is greater in this house than I am. My master has withheld nothing from me except you, because you are his wife. How then could I do such a wicked thing and sin against God?" (Gen. 39:9). Joseph taught Potiphar's wife a great lesson. Her proposed one-night stand would do more than break a wedding vow—it would break a spiritual relationship with God that Joseph valued above anything else. He said his actions would be a "sin against God."

A life of spiritual victory is a life of openness to God. Sin, breaking God's law on purpose, is like pulling the plug on your oxygen machine. You may get along for a while, but you'll finally run out of life. God made a life-saving provision through the death of His only Son, the Lord Jesus Christ. And the solution is in the receiving. "If we confess our sins, he is faithful and just and will forgive us our sins and purify us from all unrighteousness" (1 John 1:9).

If you've surrendered to temptation, ask God to forgive you. He said He would forgive. And He's never gone back on His word. A life free of guilt through faith in the promises of God's Word is a life of victory.

3. Reinforce your will power. Obviously Joseph wasn't weak in the spine. But the persistence of Potiphar's wife sent him to the "heavenly chiropractor" to keep his spine in line.

Though she spoke to Joseph day after day, he refused to go to bed with her or even be with her. One day he went into the house to attend to his duties, and none of the household servants was inside. She caught him by his cloak and said, "Come to bed with me!" But he left his cloak in her hand and ran out of the house. When she saw that he had left his cloak in her hand and had run out of the house, she called her household servants. "Look," she said to them, "this Hebrew has been brought to us to make sport of us! He came in here to sleep with me, but I screamed. When he heard me scream for help, he left his cloak beside me and ran out of the house" She kept his cloak beside her until his master came home. Then she told him this story: "That Hebrew slave you brought us came to me to make sport of me. But as soon as I screamed for help, he left his cloak beside me and ran out of the house" (*Gen. 39:10-18*).

It's a good thing that Joseph had a strong backbone. It made his running out the door easier! It wasn't a natural thing, however. Staying indoors would have been natural. Instead, he made an "unnatural" decision to flee. Let me illustrate it in this way. Dieting isn't a "natural" thing. Eating what's in plain sight is natural. When I decided to drop a few pounds, I suddenly had to make some decisions: Choosing between food groups, limiting trips to the buffet table, spending time at the gym rather than at a bake sale, and so forth. The payoff: a slimmer me—and a strengthened spine. My backbone developed along with my new eating habits. I had to make some inner decisions that would affect my health. Overcoming temptation will mean reinforcing your will power.

4. Refocus your thought life. Joseph didn't get an earthly medal for his 100-yard dash from Potiphar's master bedroom. He got a prison sentence.

When his master heard the story his wife told him, saying, "This is how your slave treated me," he burned with anger. Joseph's master took him and put him in prison, the place where the king's prisoners were confined. But while Joseph was there in the prison, the LORD was with him; he showed him kindness and granted him favor in the eyes of the prison warden. So the warden put Joseph in charge of all those held in the prison, and he was made responsible for all that was done there (*Gen. 39:19-22*).

Joseph could have easily gotten a case of the "what-ifs." But he refocused his attention on the Lord. "The LORD was with him." He refused to dwell on the temptation and chose instead to focus on the *deliverance*. That's a good example for us.

My college professor Esther Molin often shared with her class the well-known valuable analogy about temptation, that we can't keep birds from flying over our heads, but we can refuse to allow them to build a nest in our hair. You can't avoid temptation. But you can refuse to give it a long-term lease in the apartment of your heart!

5. *Rejoice in faith for God's victory.* Joseph had an edge on adversity. He was on God's side, and God was on his. "The warden paid no attention to anything under Joseph's care, because the LORD was with Joseph and gave him success in whatever he did" (v. 23). If you know going in that you have the promise of final victory, you can face just about anything. And through faith in Christ, you have just that—victory!

Rejoice in faith. It's not about *what* you face—it's *how* you face it. "For the kingdom of God is not a matter of eating and drinking, but of righteousness, peace and joy in the Holy Spirit" (Rom. 14:17). Joseph learned that when his heart was right with God, he could make the right choices. It's still true. God hasn't promised a life free of temptation. Rather, He has promised a life of victory *over* it.

Engage Brain Before Opening Mouth

Overcoming Anger

Adam and Eve had two sons. My wife, Linda, and I have two sons. As small children, our boys didn't always get along. Neither did Adam and Eve's. Adam and Eve's boys had to learn how to cope with successes, setbacks, and everything between. Ours are learning the same thing. Linda and I could have been in the same parenting class with the first family.

Our firstborn son is named Seth, our second-born Adam. (I know we got the names out of sequence, but I guess we weren't planning ahead!) Cain and Abel were the first children born to Adam and Eve and the first-ever siblings. They were also the first to act like brothers, probably even to the point of being punished for their bad behavior. They may have been the first to be sent to their room (or tent) for not doing their homework, the first to have their allowance held back for not taking out the trash, and the first to have limits set on their TV-watching (or watching shadow puppets on a cave wall). I first heard about

Cain and his brother in one of those Sunday School quizzes that no one fails. The question: "How long was Cain angry with his brother?" The answer: "As long as he was Abel!"

Seneca once said, "Anger is an acid that can do more harm to the vessel in which it is stored than to anything onto which it is poured." Anger is a *God-given* emotion that can lead either to self-preservation or to self-destruction. Anger under control can be used positively and productively. Out of control, anger can turn even the saintliest acting person into a raving lunatic!

Anger has a good side. God himself got angry (in a positive way) when people forsook holiness for heathenism.

> The Israelites did evil in the eyes of the LORD and served the Baals. They forsook the LORD, the God of their fathers, who had brought them out of Egypt. They followed and worshiped various gods of the peoples around them. They provoked the LORD to anger (*Judg. 2:11-12*).

It was a righteous anger, an anger that had redemption as its purpose. It was the same kind of anger that caused Mary's firstborn to "lay into" the folks who set up a flea market in the Temple. There wasn't any namby-pamby on Jesus' part. He was angry—righteously indignant.

> Jesus entered the temple area and drove out all who were buying and selling there. He overturned the tables of the money changers and the benches of those selling doves. "It is written," he said to them, "My house will be called a house of prayer," but you are making it a "den of robbers" (*Matt. 21:12*).

It's the *bad side* of this *good thing* called anger that we need to get a handle on. And God gives us some pretty good lessons in this chapter of His Word.

The Many Faces of Anger

Most of us don't have to worry about money lenders in the Temple (I hope!). We simply have to come to grips with things like—

- People tailgating us on the expressway.

- Folks stepping in line ahead of us at the post office.

- The IRS sending us one of those "Dear taxpayer" letters, inviting us to an auditing party for the second year in a row!

- Waiting in line at the "12 Items or Less" counter behind the dear brother who has enough groceries in his cart to feed a marching band.

- Sister Takecharge making an executive decision on the color of the carpeting in the "fellowship" hall—without asking the other members of the Decorations Committee.

Of course, Cain wasn't Abel! Two different personalities were involved. Cool-and-collected Abel did the right thing, as usual. And, as usual, Cain lost both his cool *and* his collection! Follow the story.

Adam lay with his wife Eve, and she became pregnant and gave birth to Cain. She said, "With the help of the LORD I have brought forth a man." Later she gave birth to his brother Abel. Now Abel kept flocks, and Cain worked the soil. In the course of time Cain brought some of the fruits of the soil as an offering to the LORD. But Abel brought fat portions from some of the firstborn of his flock. The LORD looked with favor on Abel and his offering, but on Cain and his offering he did not look with favor. So Cain was very angry, and his face was downcast (*Gen. 4:1-5*).

Cain was "downcast." That's Bible talk for being "up the miff tree." Quite simply, it means that he had a "two-car *grudge*" under construction! Abel had obeyed the laws of sacrifice and had brought a lamb for the offering. Cain gave the offering about as much thought as swatting a fly and took the shortcut to the temple. It wasn't that his offering wasn't adequate. It just wasn't the animal sacrifice that God had ordered. Cain disobeyed God, and when his offering was refused, he got mad at both God and Abel—so mad that he later murdered his brother (and maybe would have tried to kill God if he could have reached Him). "Now Cain said to his brother Abel, 'Let's go out to the field.' And while they were in the field, Cain attacked his brother Abel and killed him" (v. 8).

The offering thing shows us some of the faces of "bad" anger.

The first face of anger is rage. This is an uncontrollable type of anger. We only need to check the latest news headlines to see how uncontrollable anger affects a person—and those around them. "Road rage" is a modern phenomenon that results in a host of automobile accidents and deaths each year. Cain was the first offender. On the path back from the temple, his heart was filled with road rage. But the real problem wasn't that he didn't have control of the sacrifice. No, he didn't have control of *himself*! As Prov. 14:17 says, "A quick-tempered man does foolish things." Cain had a heart problem—his heart was out of rhythm with God and His Word. "Do not be like Cain, who belonged to the evil one and murdered his brother. And why did he murder him? Because his own actions were evil and his brother's were righteous" (1 John 3:12). Cain couldn't control his temper because the devil was controlling it for him!

The second face of anger is resentment. Holding a grudge is the "bad cholesterol" of human behavior. It outwardly smiles at the awards and advancements of others but burns like a torch inside.

"I deserved the *blue* ribbon."

"That was *my* promotion."

"I worked hard for that appointment. She doesn't deserve her own office!"

Resentment often has a pleasant face, but its soul is seething. Prov. 27:4 says, "Anger is cruel and fury overwhelming, but who can stand before jealousy?" Resentment may be the most insidious form of anger. It looks calm, cool, and collected on the outside, but inside, a war going on, a war that often sees such casualties as ulcers, stress, nervous disorders, anxiety, and such.

Revenge is the third face of anger. The desire to get even can be incredibly strong. I heard of two unmarried elderly sisters who had a long-standing feud that went all the way back to their teen years, when one of the ladies was asked out on a date by a young man the other lady was enamored of. On her sickbed, the offended sister told the other, "I think I'm about to die. Sister, I want you to forgive me for holding a grudge all these years."

Her sister replied. "Oh, that's all right. I forgive you." She then kissed her sister on the cheek. Before the forgiver could straighten back up, the sickly sister suddenly grabbed her arm and summoned enough strength to say, "But if I live, the war's still on!"

The writer to the Hebrew Christians warned, "See to it that no one misses the grace of God and that no bitter root grows up to cause trouble and defile many" (Heb. 12:15). I

heard Henry Brandt say at a National Association of Evangeli-
cals conference, "It's a fallacy to say that some other person
made me angry. If we become angry, it's because we already
had it in us, and we allowed someone to pull it out of us."

Cain's anger with the LORD's rejection of his sacrifice and
the acceptance of his brother's grew like a dandelion weed in
his soul (emphasis on "lion"). By the time Abel's offering had
been accepted, and even before the worship service was over,
Cain was already planning an "afterglow" for his brother. And
if Abel had only known, he wouldn't have eaten the deviled
eggs on the table!

Revenge is as contagious as full-blown chicken pox. The
wisdom writer said, "An angry man stirs up dissension, and
a hot-tempered one commits many sins" (Prov. 29:22). Revenge not only wreaks havoc on the soul but can also destroy a
church, a community, or even a nation. Look at the headlines.
The ongoing war in the Middle East, for example, is the result
of a long-time feud between warring factions that go all the
way back to Bible times.

Jesus himself wasn't immune to such a factious fallout.

On another Sabbath he went into the synagogue and
was teaching, and a man was there whose right hand was
shriveled. The Pharisees and the teachers of the law were
looking for a reason to accuse Jesus, so they watched him
closely to see if he would heal on the Sabbath. But Jesus
knew what they were thinking and said to the man with
the shriveled hand, "Get up and stand in front of everyone." So he got up and stood there. Then Jesus said to
them, "I ask you, which is lawful on the Sabbath: to do
good or to do evil, to save life or to destroy it?" He looked
around at them all, and then said to the man, "Stretch

out your hand." He did so, and his hand was completely restored. But they were furious and began to discuss with one another what they might do to Jesus (*Luke 6:6-11*).

Revengeful anger on the part of His enemies eventually took the life of the Master. It could take your life as well. Unless you determine to bury the hatchet of some grievance, the hatchet will last longer than you—and you'll be on the wrong side of the burying! Although Dr. Paul didn't have a television talk show, he had some pretty good advice: "But now you must rid yourselves of all such things as these: anger, rage, malice, slander, and filthy language from your lips" (Col. 3:8).

The Source of Anger

I'm not a psychiatrist, and I wouldn't pretend to be one—even if I stayed at that motel chain featured on the TV commercial. But I do know that God's Word isn't silent about the conditions that plague the human spirit like dry skin in winter. James, the brother of Jesus, said,

> What causes fights and quarrels among you? Don't they come from your desires that battle within you? You want something but don't get it. You kill and covet, but you cannot have what you want. You quarrel and fight. You do not have, because you do not ask God (*James 4:1-2*).

Let's break that down.

First, anger comes from a troubled spirit. "From your desires that battle within you." The problem goes all the way back to the Garden of Eden. Adam's sin ruined the tranquility of the Garden. Look at the fallout:

> To Adam he said, "Because you listened to your wife and ate from the tree about which I commanded you, 'You

must not eat of it,' "Cursed is the ground because of you; through painful toil you will eat of it all the days of your life. It will produce thorns and thistles for you, and you will eat the plants of the field. By the sweat of your brow you will eat your food until you return to the ground, since from it you were taken; for dust you are and to dust you will return" (*Gen. 3:17-19*).

Adam's conflict with God and His Word caused conflict in his heart and life. He traded peace and quiet for "thorns and thistles." It's the same for all of us. When we get "out of sorts" with God, we open ourselves to spiritual and emotional thorns and thistles that often lead to anger and cause self-inflicted wounds, or the wounding of others.

Second, anger comes from an unfulfilled desire. "You want something but don't get it." Much of the anger that builds in a "rocky" relationship, for example, comes from an unfulfilled expectation. A missed birthday card. A word not spoken. A failure to support or encourage. A lack of affection. Troubled relationships can often result from one person setting a standard that another is unable to meet.

Also, some of the anger that's carried around like a heavy antique trunk comes from unfulfilled expectations in childhood. A parent who never showed affection. A goal that couldn't be reached. A sibling who seemed to get all the attention.

We have the right to get rid of the "trunk" by laying it at the foot of the Cross; if we don't, it will be a lifelong burden.

Third, anger comes from selfishness. "You kill and covet, but you cannot have what you want." It seems that some folks never get over the "terrible twos." Their "me first" and "mine" attitude often manifests itself in rage or resentment when things don't go their way. They're a lot like the ol' boy sitting on a front porch. When one of his fellow church members came by and asked him if he was going to the church business meeting, he said, "Nope. They wouldn't listen to me the last time, so you just tell 'em that whatever they're for *this* time, I'm agin' it!"

That "my way or the highway" spirit doesn't blossom without fertilizer. When we feed our "wants" at the expense of others, it often results in angry attitudes and actions—especially when we don't get what we want.

Fourth, anger comes from a self-controlled life. "You quarrel and fight. You do not have, because you do not ask God" (James 4:2). We can't even suppress a sneeze, so why do we think we can suppress anger? A life under the control of self is a life that's subject to sudden tantrums and full-blown hissie fits. We can take all the classes we want—and some may even attend the "attitude adjustment" hour at the local lounge— but unless our emotions are under the control of the One who created them, we'll always be in danger of a blowout!

THE MANAGEMENT OF ANGER

I'm sure you've heard of athletes, movie stars, workers, or even drivers who have been sentenced by a court judge to take an "anger management" course. Thankfully, you can take a course without going through the court! Cain's angry outburst reveals some effective ways to deal with the anger problem. God quizzed Cain, "Why are you angry? Why is your face downcast? If you do what is right, will you not be accepted? But if you do not do what is right, sin is crouching at your door; it desires to have you, but you must master it" (Gen. 4:6-7). The anger management course syllabus is in these verses.

1. Confronting anger. The first class will deal with examining the causes of anger. "Then the LORD said to Cain, 'Why are you angry?'" Analyzing *why* you're angry is a first step in dealing with your anger. It may take an open and honest look back, perhaps even *way* back. What situations in your life have caused you to harbor resentment or rage? Who was the assailant? Who was the real victim? What is the *actual* result of the action or attitude that causes me pain? What is the *perceived* result?

2. Taking responsibility for anger. The second class in the course deals with the personal responsibility for anger. God said, "If you do not do what is right, sin is crouching at your door." When you look at your liability for staying angry, you'll take a giant step toward overcoming the anger problem. *What happened to you* is out of your control. But *how you reacted to what happened* has a spiritual solution. God's Word puts the monkey on our backs: "'In your anger do not sin': Do not let the sun go down while you are still angry, and do not give the devil a foothold" (Eph. 4:26). Look at those words carefully. "In your anger do not sin" (don't let *positive* anger turn to *negative* anger). "Do not let the sun go down while you are still angry" (don't let negative anger go unresolved). "Do not give the devil a foothold" (don't let the enemy of your soul take control of your emotions; instead, give them over to God).

Admitting that you're angry is a first step toward confessing it to God. And confessing your anger to God is a sure step toward His forgiveness (see 1 John 1:9).

3. Resolve your anger with others. The third class in anger management focuses on "dealing with it." God said of Cain's anger over his brother's "accepted" offering, "It desires to have you, but you must master it." In other words, "You're going to have to grab anger by the throat." How? By extending an outstretched hand! Dr. Paul had another piece of advice:

> Do not let any unwholesome talk come out of your mouths, but only what is helpful for building others up according to their needs, that it may benefit those who listen. And do not grieve the Holy Spirit of God, with whom you were sealed for the day of redemption. Get rid of all bitterness, rage and anger, brawling and slander, along with every form of malice (*Eph. 4:29-31*).

Much of your anger could be resolved by simply saying, "I'm sorry." Start with telling God you're sorry. That's the first and most important bridge that must be crossed. Anger with others puts you at odds with God. Confessing your anger to Him and enjoying the peace of His forgiveness is like eating an energy bar. It will give you enough protein and sugar to take the next, and hardest, step: Asking someone else for forgiveness. Jesus said there was an "order of worship" when it comes to resolving conflict: "If you are offering your gift at the altar and there remember that your brother has something against you, leave your gift there in front of the altar. First go and be reconciled to your brother; then come and offer your gift" (Matt. 5:23-24).

My friend Raymond McHenry often says, "Only through the power of Christ can we find the strength to lay down rocks of anger rather than reaching for more." In other words, an "empty-handed" approach to resolving conflict with others—and overcoming anger—is the best approach. Get rid of the "stuff" you're carrying in order to reach out to shake a hand in reconciliation. Cain didn't. He kept the rocks in his hand—and even might have thrown one at his brother, Abel! But that leads me to another question: Who really had rocks in his head?

Negative anger can be controlled by the sanctifying power of the Holy Spirit.

But the fruit of the Spirit is love, joy, peace, patience, kindness, goodness, faithfulness, gentleness and self-control. Against such things there is no law. Those who belong to Christ Jesus have crucified the sinful nature with its passions and desires. Since we live by the Spirit, let us keep in step with the Spirit. Let us not become conceited, provoking and envying each other (*Gal. 5:22-26*).

Using Anger for Good

Author and professor of pastoral care Daniel Bagby wrote, "Anger, in the prayerful hands of the people of God, can rise to be a channel of concern. And by the grace of God, with patience and sensitivity, it can become a constructive force for God."[1] There is a positive and powerful force of anger that can work for good in society and in the Church.

God tightened the screws in interrogating Cain. You can almost see the perspiration bead on the forehead of the guilty brother. The Judge of all the earth began to ask some probing questions to the one who stood before His bench:

Then the LORD said to Cain, "Where is your brother Abel?" "I don't know," he replied. "Am I my brother's keeper?" The LORD said, "What have you done? Listen! Your brother's blood cries out to me from the ground. Now you are under a curse and driven from the ground, which opened its mouth to receive your brother's blood from your hand. When you work the ground, it will no longer yield its crops for you. You will be a restless wanderer on the earth" (*Gen. 4:9-12*).

Cain waited for the gavel to fall. He thought it was the end for him. But God, the righteous Judge, saw it as a beginning. The story continues:

> Cain said to the LORD, "My punishment is more than I can bear. Today you are driving me from the land, and I will be hidden from your presence; I will be a restless wanderer on the earth, and whoever finds me will kill me." But the LORD said to him, "Not so; if anyone kills Cain, he will suffer vengeance seven times over." Then the LORD put a mark on Cain so that no one who found him would kill him (*Gen. 4:13-15*).

God was angry at Cain's actions, but He still loved him. God's anger was a redemptive anger. He used it as a force for good in Cain's life and in the lives of all who would read the biblical story.

Let me share examples of ways that positive (good) anger can be used for the welfare of others.

1. Anger can be used to fight the spread of immorality. Nearly a million members strong, the Parents' Television Council, whose advisory board members include such public figures as Pat Boone, James Dobson, Michael Medved, and Donald Wildmon, have taken on the media. Developing their own TV rating system, they continue to warn parents about the immoral content of programs. Their stand against indecency over the airwaves comes from a positive anger over what they see and hear.

2. Anger can be used to fight political and social injustice. Christian relief organizations such as World Hope International have joined forces with secular organizations around the world to stand against the slave trafficking of women and children in the sex industry. In countries where children are sold for $100 or less, the positive anger of those who have witnessed such crimes against humanity have caused them to marshal volunteers and raise multiplied thousands of dollars to bring traffickers to justice, and to provide resettlement and care for those who have been enslaved.

3. Anger can be a force for positive change. In one sense, the great revivalist movements of the past and present have been sparked by one or more persons who have been positively angry about the complacency of the Church.

4. Anger can fortify personal weakness. History records superhuman feats of strengths, from lifting automobiles off the injured to breaking down doors to free someone from a burning building. Someone was in danger—including a loved one or friend—and nothing would stop the rescuer from making the rescue, including the fact that he or she was small in stature or weak in physical strength. The sheer anger of the threatening situation caused the person to draw from an unseen well and put his or her own life on the line to save another.

The problem of anger is an ever-present reality. Now's the time to place your anger at the foot of the Cross and allow the Spirit of Christ to control your mouth and your mind.

Sometimes I'm My Own Worst Enemy

Overcoming Inadequacy

It's an old joke, but it strikes home. A man went to a psychiatrist because he had feelings of inferiority. After several sessions, the patient asked the doctor for an update: "Why do I still feel so inadequate?" The psychiatrist replied, "Well, Jake, as far as I can tell, it's because you really are!"

The patient would have been in worse shape if he had tried to put out a thorn bush that had an eternal flame burning inside. Ask Moses. He was in the desert outback, on 40 years of probation for defending a countryman who had taken a beating at the hands of the enemy. In the prime of life, Moses had been raised in a gated community of Egypt, went to an Ivy League school, and had career advantages that others would only dream of. But instead of leading a Hebrew corporation, he was tending a flock of matted and smelly sheep.

Then, what started out as an ordinary day for a shepherd turned into D-day:

Now Moses was tending the flock of Jethro his father-in-law, the priest of Midian, and he led the flock to the far side of the desert and came to Horeb, the mountain of God. There the angel of the LORD appeared to him in flames of fire from within a bush. Moses saw that though the bush was on fire it did not burn up. So Moses thought, "I will go over and see this strange sight—why the bush does not burn up." When the LORD saw that he had gone over to look, God called to him from within the bush, "Moses! Moses!" And Moses said, "Here I am." "Do not come any closer," God said. "Take off your sandals, for the place where you are standing is holy ground." Then he said, "I am the God of your father, the God of Abraham, the God of Isaac and the God of Jacob." At this, Moses hid his face, because he was afraid to look at God.

The LORD said, "I have indeed seen the misery of my people in Egypt. I have heard them crying out because of their slave drivers, and I am concerned about their suffering. So I have come down to rescue them from the hand of the Egyptians and to bring them up out of that land into a good and spacious land, a land flowing with milk and honey—the home of the Canaanites, Hittites, Amorites, Perizzites, Hivites and Jebusites. And now the cry of the Israelites has reached me, and I have seen the way the Egyptians are oppressing them. So now, go. I am sending you to Pharaoh to bring my people the Israelites out of Egypt" (*Exod. 3:1-10*).

God had a corporate leadership position for Moses. And He used a pretty spectacular setting to conduct the interview. Moses' reaction? "Moses hid his face." Of course, if we were mountain climbing on Mt. Horeb and suddenly heard God speak to us from a burning bush, we might play a little hide and seek ourselves! But Moses' first reaction became a link to several others. Moses, one of the great leaders of all time, had to overcome feelings of inadequacy.

That's important to us, because sooner or later we'll face our own "burning bush" in the outback of our own desert. Oswald Chambers said, "All through history God has chosen and used nobodies because their unusual dependence upon Him made possible the unique display of His power and grace."[1] We'll come to a place where we'll have to make a "nobody" decision as to whether or not we have the goods to do what God wants us to do. Moses had a dialogue with the Lord that gives us some great insights on overcoming our own feelings of inadequacy. In Exod. 3—4 I see *five excuses that Moses gave God when faced with a leadership decision*. And I also see five answers that God gave. In between that hillside talk and the parting of the Red Sea, which Moses accomplished with the wave of his shepherd's staff, he faced his inadequacies— and overcame them by the promises and power of God. The conversation is important. Whether we're called to be the CEO of a major corporation or to answer some childish questions around a hurried breakfast before the school bus arrives, we'll have times when we feel like hiding our face, as if we're totally inadequate for the job. Look at Moses' excuses and God's answers.

I Don't Have the Credibility

"But Moses said to God, 'Who am I that I should go to Pharaoh and bring the Israelites out of Egypt?'" (Exod. 3:11). Moses faced his calling with a question. That's not unlike some of us. He seemed to be saying, "God, why use me? On a scale of 1 to 10, I'm in a negative-1 position!" Perhaps he had a lapse of faith and thought that the God of the universe was suffering from memory loss.

- "God, if you remember, I'm doing time in the desert."
- "God, if you remember, my only athletic skill is wind-surfing in a basket on the Nile River."
- "God, if you remember, I'm not even a rightful heir of the royal family. I'm a foster child."
- "God, if you remember, my leadership skills are so rusty I couldn't lead a one-sheep animal parade."

Moses made his credibility case before the Creator. But the Creator wasn't that impressed. Look at God's answer. His comeback turned the desert-dweller's heart to mush: "I will be with you. And this will be the sign to you that it is I who have sent you: When you have brought the people out of Egypt, you will worship God on this mountain" (v. 12).

First, God gave Moses a spiritual shot in the arm that was loaded with a promise: "I will be with you." In other words, "*My* credibility is *your* credibility! You'll be wearing my ID badge!" When Jesus sent His disciples to turn the world upside down, some of them must have left the meeting with some similar doubts in their mind. But they had one thing that gave them an eternal confidence: The promise of Christ's presence.

Then Jesus came to them and said, "All authority in heaven and on earth has been given to me. Therefore go and make disciples of all nations, baptizing them in the name of the Father and of the Son and of the Holy Spirit, and teaching them to obey everything I have commanded you. And surely I am with you always, to the very end of the age" (*Matt. 28:18-20*).

Second, God added an interesting addendum: "When you have brought the people out of Egypt, you will worship God on this mountain." Suppose He would have said "If" or "Perhaps." It would have made everything different. "When" gave it a stamp of authority. God seemed to say to Moses, "When it's over—and it will be—I'll bring you right back here to the 'scene of the *whine'* as a triumphant hero. This mountain—right here! Right where you said, 'Who am I that I should go . . . ?'"

You can overcome a sense of inadequacy in the very same way. Focus on *whose you are* instead of what you're called to do. You're God's person for God's assignment in God's presence. You're wearing God's ID badge—and that will get you through the toughest places with the highest level of credibility.

Notice his second excuse.

I Don't Have the Knowledge

Like some Christians today, Moses assumed that the people he would attempt to lead would know more about the Scriptures than he. He felt like a dropout from preschool! "Moses said to God, 'Suppose I go to the Israelites and say to them, "The God of your fathers has sent me to you," and they ask me, "What is his name?" Then what shall I tell them?'" (Exod. 3:13). You can almost envision Moses being on the television game show *Jeopardy* and saying, "Alex, I'll take 'The Almighty' for $400." The game show host asks the question, Moses has the buzzer in his hand, the answer is revealed, and he suddenly draws a blank. He couldn't remember his name if it were written on a cue card in front of him!

Moses forgot what he knew about God. All he could remember was the fact that he had stage fright. And there would be over a million Israelites in the audience (600,000 men, plus women and children) who would expect him to have all the answers. I've had the same feeling; only it was an audience of one instead of one million: my college professor. "Stan, give me the Greek word for 'love.'" I couldn't even give him the Greek word for "salad"—as in Greek salad. I knew the answer, but the pressure of the moment put an excise tax on my memory, and all my brain cells congealed like lime Jell-O! I felt as small as the time I got an autographed jersey from Houston Rockets center Dikembe Mutumbo. My 5' 8" frame stood next to the 7' 2" professional basketball player. I felt a lot like Zacchaeus!

Moses was on that kind of spot. He had a tall assignment, and he was short on courage. But Moses forgot who God is. He needed a reminder that God is the source of knowledge. Every fact or philosophy he would need to lead women and children and their dads or husbands would be supplied when he needed it. He would have all the answers on spiritual flash cards—and the Holy Spirit would reveal the answers to his spirit.

God not only let Moses know that He would fill in the gaps —He gave him a theology lesson as well. He said to Moses,

I AM WHO I AM. This is what you are to say to the Israelites: "I AM has sent me to you." God also said to Moses, "Say to the Israelites, 'The LORD, the God of your fathers—the God of Abraham, the God of Isaac and the God of Jacob—has sent me to you.' This is my name forever, the name by which I am to be remembered from generation to generation" (*Exod. 3:14-15*).

Moses wasn't afraid that he wouldn't know some password for the Almighty; rather, he wanted the people to know that he knew *who* God is and *what* He can do. "I AM," the all-sufficient Jehovah God, was sending him to lead the people.

God has a good name. Often taken in vain, and often used flippantly by clergy and laity alike, God's name is without equal. It's a name of power, holiness, justice, mercy, love, grace, and whatever else may describe His infinite character or characteristics. Moses had only to remind the Israelites of his "family name."

And you may need a reminder as well. You may come across a difficult people—or a difficult situation—and forget that you are there as a representative of the family of God. In fact you were a foster child, but God adopted you through faith in Christ and gave you His name. "To all who received him, to those who believed in his name, he gave the right to become children of God" (John 1:12).

Think of the "power" names in our society. Some family names mean instant recognition or status for the children bearing them. Now multiply that times infinity, and you have an idea of the adequacy that comes from being in God's family! "Moses, go tell the people that Jehovah has sent you!"

But God took Moses a step farther:

> Go, assemble the elders of Israel and say to them, "The LORD, the God of your fathers—the God of Abraham, Isaac and Jacob—appeared to me and said: I have watched over you and have seen what has been done to you in Egypt. And I have promised to bring you up out of your misery in Egypt into the land of the Canaanites, Hittites, Amorites, Perizzites, Hivites and Jebusites—a land flowing with milk and honey" (*Exod. 3:16-17*).

God wanted Moses to understand that with the knowledge of His name, he also had the knowledge of His provision.

James said, "If any of you lacks wisdom, he should ask God, who gives generously to all without finding fault, and it will be given to him" (James 1:5).

God has closed the knowledge gap for you. It isn't a matter of your grade-point average or even your degrees—or lack thereof. If you know God, you're "in the know." Rest in His wisdom. Take advantage of the instruction of His Word. Ask His advice in prayer. Trust the Spirit-filled counsel of His saints.

There's another excuse.

I Don't Have the Experience

Moses' third excuse pitted him against the elders of Israel. He was a rookie with a record—the kind listed at the post office, not the kind that reaches the top of the charts. While the spiritual and administrative leaders of Israel were calling the shots, Moses was calling sheep in the desert. "Moses answered, 'What if they do not believe me or listen to me and say, "The Lord did not appear to you"?'" (Exod. 4:1). In other words, what if they think the burning bush incident was just a tall tale? After all, he was a teenager compared to the aged sages of Israel.

New Testament pastor Timothy must have had the same quiver in his voice. His mentor, the apostle Paul, set the record straight: "Don't let anyone look down on you because you are young, but set an example for the believers in speech, in life, in love, in faith and in purity" (1 Tim. 4:12).

I know somewhat how Moses and Timothy must have felt. I was a teenager when I preached my first sermon, and in my early 20s when I pastored my first church. Some members of the audience had handkerchiefs that were older than I was. And I think there was a time or two when the members of my church board secretly talked about taking me out behind the church and giving me a "whooppin'" for all my newfangled ideas!

Moses tried to get up the courage to talk about the burning bush incident—and courage to talk about his call to replace the leaders of Israel with himself. "What if they do not believe me?" Moses felt about as adequate as a wet noodle. He was going to tell those seasoned veterans that he was their new leader.

God answered the question with an object lesson.

Then the LORD said to him, "What is that in your hand?" "A staff," he replied. The LORD said, "Throw it on the ground." Moses threw it on the ground and it became a snake, and he ran from it. Then the LORD said to him, "Reach out your hand and take it by the tail." So Moses reached out and took hold of the snake and it turned back into a staff in his hand. "This," said the LORD, "is so that they may believe that the LORD, the God of their fathers— the God of Abraham, the God of Isaac and the God of Jacob—has appeared to you" (*Exod. 4:2-5*).

In one sense, God was teaching Moses that not all miracles happened in the past. In another, God was teaching Moses that even common things can be used for an uncommon purpose. Though Moses felt inadequate due to his experience, God was illustrating that adequacy is in higher hands than his.

Brother Moses was a lot like some of us, though. The first thing he did when God showed him a miracle was to run from it. Burning bushes. Shepherd staffs turning to snakes. What will the media think? Far-right conservatism? Lunatic fringe Christianity? Fact is, the foundation of our faith is built from the bricks of the supernatural. We believe in people created from dust, arks floating on 40-day floods, prophets ascending to the skies in heavenly flying machines, great fish feeding on great preachers, a child born to a virgin, empty tombs, dead people walking, tongues of fire dancing on disciple heads.

Modern pastors weren't the first to have staffs that could work miracles. Moses was. (Only his didn't need health insurance or two-week vacations!) By the way, God's "firsts" are still possible. He isn't limited by time or space. And neither is His adequacy. How could you doubt your credentials of experience when you serve an *eternal* God?

Moses looked at his abilities and offered another excuse.

I Don't Have the Gifts

Moses loved God's sense of humor, but he didn't get the joke. Moses was to give marching orders to a million or more people, and he had a speech problem. Either he couldn't think fast enough to talk, or he had an impediment. Either way, he didn't feel adequate to speak to the masses. "Moses said to the Lord, 'O Lord, I have never been eloquent, neither in the past nor since you have spoken to your servant. I am slow of speech and tongue'" (Exod. 4:10). Who knows? It could have taken him 40 days and 40 nights just to say, "Move 'em out!" And what if the command had to be passed all the way to the back of the crowd of Israelites? "What did he say?" By the time the command reached the last row, it could have sounded like the results of one of those parlor games of "gossip."

"He said, 'I have the gout!'"

It could have been a long winter, and Moses knew it. He was called to communicate—and he had a broken communicator. But he's not the first to doubt whether spiritual gifts were handed out in an equitable way. Some have watched an evangelist, or some other public speaker, and said inwardly, *I wish I could talk like that.*

Others have listened as musical melodies seemed to float from a grand piano and said, "I would love to play a piano." Still others watch religious television and almost covet the televised teacher's explanation of a Scripture passage and wonder, *How come she got all the gifts?* No, Moses wasn't the only player on the field who wished he could hit home runs.

But God gave the same answer to Moses as he gives to us: "The LORD said to him, 'Who gave man his mouth? Who makes him deaf or mute? Who gives him sight or makes him blind? Is it not I, the LORD? Now go; I will help you speak and will teach you what to say" (Exod. 4:11-12). In other words, "I'm in charge of the gifts here!" The God who loved the world so much that He gave His only Son gives us everything we *need* to do everything He *expects.*

Spiritual gifts come factory-installed and are activated when a person is born again.

> Now to each one the manifestation of the Spirit is given for the common good. To one there is given through the Spirit the message of wisdom, to another the message of knowledge by means of the same Spirit, to another faith by the same Spirit, to another gifts of healing by that one Spirit, to another miraculous powers, to another prophecy, to another distinguishing between spirits, to another speaking in different kinds of tongues, and to still another the interpretation of tongues. All these are the work of one and the same Spirit, and he gives them to each one, just as he determines.

> The body is a unit, though it is made up of many parts; and though all its parts are many, they form one body. So

it is with Christ. For we were all baptized by one Spirit into one body—whether Jews or Greeks, slave or free—and we were all given the one Spirit to drink. Now the body is not made up of one part but of many. If the foot should say, "Because I am not a hand, I do not belong to the body," it would not for that reason cease to be part of the body. And if the ear should say, "Because I am not an eye, I do not belong to the body," it would not for that reason cease to be part of the body. If the whole body were an eye, where would the sense of hearing be? If the whole body were an ear, where would the sense of smell be? But in fact God has arranged the parts in the body, every one of them, just as he wanted them to be (*1 Cor. 12:7-18*).

The bottom line: God has given you the ability to do whatever He expects you to do. You may need to work on that ability—practice it within the community of faith—but you have the gifts. And, of course, spiritual gifts differ. Thank the Lord! If everyone had the gift of preaching, the auditorium would look empty, and the platform would need renovation.

What was the instruction to Moses? Notice: "Who gave man his mouth? . . . Is it not I, the LORD?" The problem isn't bigger than the *Provider*! God doesn't have any inadequacy. Our adequacies become inadequacies only when we focus on *them* instead of *Him*.

Second, spiritual gifts are developed on the field, not in the stands. "Now *go*; I will help you speak and will teach you what to say" (Exod. 4:12, emphasis added). There's an old saying that describes folks who have a spiritual gift wish list: "If wishes were horses, then beggars would ride." Some may even have a spiritual gift registry at a local discount store. But spiritually, that's a waste of time. God has already gifted you for the good of the Church—not for your good. Listen to Paul: "Since you are eager to have spiritual gifts, try to excel in gifts that build up the church" (1 Cor. 14:12).

There's one last excuse.

I Don't Have the Courage

God taught Moses everything he needed to know about adequacy—and he still didn't get it! "But Moses said, 'O Lord, please send someone else to do it'" (Exod. 4:13). Now before you start shaking your head and pointing fingers at Moses, remember the time you were given an assignment that appeared to be a 500-pound gorilla with a toothache. Remember when the homecoming queen came through the door of your 25th high school reunion looking like an "after" model in a weight-loss advertisement. Remember the time you were suddenly asked to take the junior high Sunday School class.

Overcoming inadequacy not only needs a game plan—it needs a game. It needs to be on the field. It needs to run the plays that Coach Jesus put on the whiteboard of the Word. "Now go: I will help you speak and will teach you what to say" (Exod. 4:12).

You've heard the expression "That's enough to try the patience of Job." But there's a higher level than that of the Old Testament character who didn't lose his cool even when he had lost just about everything else. The Bible says we can try the patience of *God*. Notice that Exod. 4:14 says, "Then the Lord's anger burned against Moses . . ."

Now, I'm going to be careful of my theology here. God obviously has more patience and mercy than His creation; otherwise He would have pronounced judgment on those who have blasphemed His name and His word with their attitudes and actions.

But God is a sovereign judge. And He has the power and authority to say, "That's enough!" The early Christians in Rome got a letter from the apostle Paul that gave a stern warning about pushing the envelope.

The wrath of God is being revealed from heaven against all the godlessness and wickedness of men who suppress the truth by their wickedness, since what may be known about God is plain to them, because God has made it plain to them. For since the creation of the world God's invisible qualities—his eternal power and divine nature—have been clearly seen, being understood from what has been made, so that men are without excuse. For although they knew God, they neither glorified him as God nor gave thanks to him, but their thinking became futile and their foolish hearts were darkened. Although they claimed to be wise, they became fools and exchanged the glory of the immortal God for images made to look like mortal man and birds and animals and reptiles. *Therefore God gave them over* in the sinful desires of their hearts to sexual impurity for the degrading of their bodies with one another (*Rom. 1:18-24, emphasis added*).

Let's be clear—God's mercy can never be exhausted. It doesn't just run through our lives like a river—it's more like an ocean. As long as we keep on seeking Him, even in the feelings of our inadequacy, He will still help us. He helped Moses after he asked to be excused from the table of service. God seemed to sigh and then gave Moses one more bit of help.

It's a defining word on God's support for those who feel helpless.

> Then the LORD's anger burned against Moses and he said, "What about your brother, Aaron the Levite? I know he can speak well. He is already on his way to meet you, and his heart will be glad when he sees you. You shall speak to him and put words in his mouth; I will help both of you speak and will teach you what to do. He will speak to the people for you, and it will be as if he were your mouth and as if you were God to him" (*Exod. 4:14-16*).

Aaron, Moses' assistant—the next step in God's favor to Moses. "He is already on the way." I like that! God's answers are already on the way.

So here's the plan:

- Identify your fears
- Change your thinking about them
- Let God take up the slack

Cervantes said, "Love not what you are, but what you may become." That's pretty good advice, but there's better: "God is able to make all grace abound to you, so that in all things at all times, having all that you need, you will abound in every good work" (2 Cor. 9:8). Amen!

While You're Waiting, God Is Working

Overcoming Doubt

N o *doubt* you've heard of Thomas the disciple. He was the follower of Christ who had the dubious distinction of second-guessing every living proof of Jesus' resurrection—in person!

On the evening of that first day of the week, when the disciples were together, with the doors locked for fear of the Jews, Jesus came and stood among them and said, "Peace be with you!" After he said this, he showed them his hands and side. The disciples were overjoyed when they saw the Lord. Again Jesus said, "Peace be with you! As the Father has sent me, I am sending you." And with that he breathed on them and said, "Receive the Holy Spirit. If you forgive anyone his sins, they are forgiven; if you do not forgive them, they are not forgiven."

Now Thomas (called Didymus), one of the Twelve, was not with the disciples when Jesus came. So the other disciples told him, "We have seen the Lord!" But he said to them, "Unless I see the nail marks in his hands and put my finger where the nails were, and put my hand into his side, I will not believe it."

A week later his disciples were in the house again and Thomas was with them. Though the doors were locked, Jesus came and stood among them and said, "Peace be with you!" Then he said to Thomas, "Put your finger here; see my hands. Reach out your hand and put it into my side. Stop doubting and believe." Thomas said to him, "My Lord and my God!" (*John 20:19-28*).

The apostle Peter also had a bout with doubt. How did he go from being "overjoyed" to being overwhelmed? It happened later on in his ministry—his vibrant and effective ministry. The lessons that Jesus' trusted disciple learned about himself and about overcoming doubtful situations are like spiritual multivitamins for the soul.

The disciples were making a huge impact on their culture. Lives were being changed by their gospel message. Their testimonies drew people to them—and subsequently to their Lord.

Then the devil commissioned his goon squad.

It was about this time that King Herod arrested some who belonged to the church, intending to persecute them. He had James, the brother of John, put to death with the sword. When he saw that this pleased the Jews, he proceeded to seize Peter also. This happened during the Feast of Unleavened Bread. After arresting him, he put him in prison, handing him over to be guarded by four squads of four soldiers each. Herod intended to bring him out for public trial after the Passover (*Acts 12:1-4*).

Suddenly the great man of faith, who had once jumped into the water and walked on the waves toward Jesus, was at a barbershop quartet convention ("four squads of four soldiers each"). The situation sent a slight chill up and down the once-strong spine of the disciple who was in Christ's inner circle. These quartet singers may have had their bow ties and straw hats on, but they were singing out of tune!

Peter was also having a difficult time carrying the harmony part. The situation was about as hopeful as a car wash fund-raiser on a rainy day. But Peter had been on the ledge before. And he had always found a way back to the safety of his Savior. Let's take a closer look at this predicament and see how the God-solution played itself out. It has some lessons that we can use when the doubts roll in like a thunderstorm in Oklahoma. Notice six steps to overcoming doubt in Acts 12:

1. PRAY WITH PASSION

"Peter was kept in prison, but the church was earnestly praying to God for him" (v. 5). Prayer is always the first line of defense; and it is one of the most effective means for dealing with a case of the *doubts*.

Some use up their prayer quotas at lunchtime. They suffer spiritual burnout with a 15-word blessing often hidden behind hand-shielded eyes, and uttered so softly that the angels have to lean over the banisters of heaven to hear it: *God is great. God is good. Let us thank Him for our food. Amen.*

Others use their lunchtime prayers as a warm-up for the main course. Peter was not only a man of prayer—he also hung out with major league *pray-ers*. And this was a major league circumstance. Years spent on a prayer "farm team," learning the *ropes* of righteousness, practicing their prayer pitches, and learning how to hit toward the upper deck would soon pay off for the team. It was time for them to stand on the top steps of the dugout in the "Bigs." It was time to do some holy hollering! One of their own was two strikes down, and the pitcher/devil had just thrown a dangerous bean ball, aiming to put the disciple onto the injured reserve list—or worse, sending him packing for home.

Prayer is seldom convenient, but it's always *convincing*. "The prayer of a righteous man is powerful and effective" (James 5:16). The prayer team could have set a "For Sale" sign up in front of their house church. They could have crossed Peter off their pastoral candidate list and started looking for one who wasn't serving jail time. But they didn't. Peter the apostle was a servant of the Lord, and he was in trouble. They assembled the prayer team and played a double-header against hell's best. And they were so busy praying that they didn't have time to doubt whether the apostle would ever see daylight again.

Prayer is an effective tool for dealing with *the doubts*:

- It focuses on God instead of the problem.
- It meets fear with faith.
- It helps us understand that we are not alone.
- It recalls past victories.
- It mentally takes us away from the threatening situation.

But prayer and doubt don't belong in the same worship service. Jesus instructed, "I tell you the truth, if anyone says to this mountain, 'Go, throw yourself into the sea,' and does not doubt in his heart but believes that what he says will happen, it will be done for him" (Mark 11:23). "And does not doubt."

The children of Israel didn't make a habit of practicing that principle. At one point on their journey, they pulled over to the roadside and had a pity party. Their leader, Moses, was in the lead car of the caravan when someone started a cell phone-a-thon, complaining that the egg salad sandwiches, potato chips, and bottled water were running low. And besides, they spotted some boulders on their in-dash navigation system that could possibly have some enemy troops behind them.

That night all the people of the community raised their voices and wept aloud. All the Israelites grumbled against Moses and Aaron, and the whole assembly said to them, "If only we had died in Egypt! Or in this desert! Why is the LORD bringing us to this land only to let us fall by the sword? Our wives and children will be taken as plunder. Wouldn't it be better for us to go back to Egypt?" And they said to each other, "We should choose a leader and go back to Egypt" (*Num. 14:1-4*).

Along with forgetting they already had a leader, they overlooked a few other things:

- The trip through the Red Sea on dry ground (Exod. 13:18).
- The cloud that guided them through the wilderness (Exod. 13:21).
- The column of fire that lit their travels by night (Exod. 13:22).
- The manna that fell from heaven to feed them (Deut. 8:16).
- The bitter waters that turned sweet (Exod. 15:23-25).

So Moses parked the caravan in the parking lot of a nearby mall and circled the saints for a business meeting. One dear lady may have stepped forward, swung her scarf threateningly around her neck, and reminded Brother Moses that he had already sent a committee on ahead to scope out the land of Canaan, Israel's future home, and that the committee had come back with a trunk full of doubt in their Toyota. Instead of seeing the wealth, beauty, and abundance of the place, they saw the worst.

They came back to Moses and Aaron and the whole Israelite community at Kadesh in the Desert of Paran. There they reported to them and to the whole assembly and showed them the fruit of the land. They gave Moses this account: "We went into the land to which you sent us, and it does flow with milk and honey! Here is its fruit. But the people who live there are powerful, and the cities are fortified and very large. We even saw descendants of Anak there. The Amalekites live in the Negev; the Hittites, Jebusites and Amorites live in the hill country; and the Canaanites live near the sea and along the Jordan." Then Caleb silenced the people before Moses and said, "We should go up and take possession of the land, for we can certainly do it."

But the men who had gone up with him said, "We can't attack those people; they are stronger than we are." And they spread among the Israelites a bad report about the land they had explored. They said, "The land we explored devours those living in it. All the people we saw there are of great size. We saw the Nephilim there (the descendants of Anak come from the Nephilim). We seemed like grasshoppers in our own eyes, and we looked the same to them" (*Num. 13:26-33*).

Two members of the committee, Caleb and his buddy Joshua, were the only ones in the bunch who had read a

John Maxwell book. They were thinking positive and making long-range leadership plans, while the rest of the committee members were as negative as a frozen turkey on Thanksgiving eve! The majority of the committee came to one conclusion: "We can't!" The two who eventually turned the whole caravan around had another conclusion: "*God* can!"

What will your report be? Will you look for the miracle in the mess? Will you "take your burden to the Lord and leave it there," as one songwriter suggested? Will you believe the promises of God in spite of the negatives? If so, your prayer time will be a positive step toward overcoming doubt.

There's another important step visible in the apostle Peter's jail incident.

STEADFASTLY TRUST IN GOD

The night before Herod was to bring him to trial, Peter was sleeping between two soldiers, bound with two chains, and sentries stood guard at the entrance. Suddenly an angel of the Lord appeared and a light shone in the cell. He struck Peter on the side and woke him up. "Quick, get up!" he said, and the chains fell off Peter's wrists" (*Acts 12:6-7*).

Notice several things.

First, Peter had given the situation over to the Lord. "The night before . . . Peter was sleeping" (v. 6). Sleeping? Some of us would have been wide-eyed awake, counting tigers instead of sheep. Not the apostle. He had been in the boat when Jesus calmed the waves. He had stood by the bedside as Jesus rebuked his mother-in-law's fever. He had even watched the Master put the dismembered ear of a Roman soldier back in place—the one that Peter had sliced off with his Swiss Army knife the night Jesus was arrested. He knew the Lord wouldn't fail him now.

Second, the armed forces of earth are no match for the armies of heaven. "Peter was sleeping between two soldiers, bound with two chains, and sentries stood guard at the entrance" (v. 6). Herod was clueless! He thought that a few enemy soldiers and a couple of chains could keep a good man down. He totally underestimated the power of God for the predicaments of His children. But Herod isn't alone in trusting natural solutions. Many folks have made their plans for getting out of a tough situation but forgetting the most important factor: God's power.

"Trust God" is often put in the same category as "Have a nice day." But the end result is as different as 99-cent specials in fast-food restaurants. "Have a nice day" suggests doing everything in *your* power to deal with the delights and dangers of living on the planet. "Trust God" is putting the heavens to work in making sure that a bad day turns into a "nice day."

The psalmist marked the difference: "Some trust in chariots and some in horses, but we trust in the name of the LORD our God" (Ps. 20:7). How many chariots and horses do you have lined up? There will never be enough. You'll need to "trust in the name of the LORD"—in His power and authority—to overcome doubtful circumstances and doubt itself.

Third, God's deliverance is always on schedule. "Suddenly an angel of the Lord appeared" (Acts 12:7). The master plan for Peter's deliverance had been put into place eons before the Roman soldiers had read the Miranda Rights to the apostle. "You have the right to remain silent. Anything you say can and will be used against you in a court of law. You have the right to speak to an attorney and to have an attorney present during any questioning. If you cannot afford a lawyer, one will be provided for you at government expense."

I like the spiritual implications. We have a right to remain silent. Doubts often come from a well of words that are drawn in tough situations. We have a right to trust God and keep silent, instead of complaining.

We also have the right to speak to an attorney—our advocate. "My dear children, I write this to you so that you will not sin. But if anybody does sin, we have one who speaks to the Father in our defense—Jesus Christ, the Righteous One" (1 John 2:1). Our Attorney is seated next to the Father in heaven, pleading our cause.

Some courts appoint an attorney, one who officially represents the accused. Jesus promised a spiritual "court-appointed attorney," a Counselor, the Holy Spirit.

> If you love me, you will obey what I command. And I will ask the Father, and he will give you another Counselor to be with you forever—the Spirit of truth. The world cannot accept him, because it neither sees him nor knows him. But you know him, for he lives with you and will be in you (*John 14:15-17*).

That certainly puts a damper on doubt! Heaven cares enough about your case to have a Counselor at your side 24/7.

Fourth, Peter's deliverance was dynamic, not static. The angel "struck Peter on the side and woke him up. 'Quick, get up!' he said, and the chains fell off Peter's wrists" (Acts 12:7). If you're going to trust the Lord for overcoming your doubt, you might as well understand that there may be some "unexpecteds" along the way, some hurts ("struck") and some awakenings ("woke him up"). You'll also need to understand that faith is "in process." The chains fell off *during* the event.

There's another step,

BECOME RADICALLY OBEDIENT

> Then the angel said to him, "Put on your clothes and sandals." And Peter did so. "Wrap your cloak around you and follow me," the angel told him. Peter followed him out of the prison, but he had no idea that what the angel was doing was really happening; he thought he was seeing a vision. They passed the first and second guards and came to the iron gate leading to the city. It opened for them by itself, and they went through it. When they had walked the length of one street, suddenly the angel left him (*Acts 12:8-10*).

Obedience was primary to Peter's deliverance. Look carefully:

- **Peter obeyed no matter what the details were.** "Put on your clothes and sandals" (v. 8). Taking time for the sandals was a stretch. If you're escaping a company of guards in the middle of the night, you might be tempted to go barefoot and skip the time it would take to tie your sandals. Obedience always submits to God's time.

- **Peter obeyed no matter what the unknowns were.** "Peter followed him out of the prison, but he had no idea that what the angel was doing was really happening" (v. 9). The important thing for the apostle was to simply do what heaven's representative said, whether he understood the process or not. Obedience doesn't question.

- **Peter obeyed no matter how many steps it took.** "They passed the first and second guards and came to the iron gate leading to the city. It opened for them by itself, and they went through it" (v. 10). Each step, each guard, and each obstacle was a journey to deliverance. Obedience is willing to follow God's path.

Peter's attitude also helped him overcome his doubts and reveals another important step.

Develop a Thankful Heart

"Then Peter came to himself and said, 'Now I know without a doubt that the Lord sent his angel and rescued me from Herod's clutches and from everything the Jewish people were anticipating'" (v. 11). The apostle didn't say, "Well, I pulled *that* one off!" No, he humbly gave praise where it was due: to the Lord. Thanksgiving is an antidote for doubt, whether you're still "in the prison" or have "passed the gate." Believing that God has or will deliver you from a problem, and praising Him for it, gives you spiritual strength for the next situation.

"I will praise you forever for what you have done; in your name I will hope, for your name is good. I will praise you in the presence of your saints" (Ps. 52:9). The expression "Give credit where credit is due" doesn't have a nobler setting than in a situation like the apostle's. A thankful heart is a heart that has doubt on the defensive.

When you begin to praise God—even when you don't see obvious answers—you're adding gospel gasoline to the fire of your faith. One thing I remember about English class was the need to get the "tense" right—past tense, present tense, future tense, past perfect, future perfect, and so on. It's amazing that I've been writing for over 20 years, and no one has asked me to come to his or her city or nation to do a seminar on the "tenses." But it's been my privilege to tell people in churches and convention centers around the world how they can perfect their tenses—as in tensions.

Begin to praise the Lord in spite of the problem. It'll cause your doubts to get on the Internet and start looking for discounts on air travel!

Notice another step.

CONFESS YOUR WEAKNESS

> When this had dawned on him, he went to the house of Mary the mother of John, also called Mark, where many people had gathered and were praying. Peter knocked at the outer entrance, and a servant girl named Rhoda came to answer the door. When she recognized Peter's voice, she was so overjoyed she ran back without opening it and exclaimed, "Peter is at the door!" "You're out of your mind," they told her. When she kept insisting that it was so, they said, "It must be his angel" (*Acts 12:12-15*).

Doubt is obviously contagious. It's too bad that health clinics don't offer a "doubt vaccine;" but that's where the Church comes in. The apostle Peter didn't keep the miracle to himself. He had overcome dungeons, doubts, and Herod's armed guards. An angel of the Lord had invaded his prison cell, punched him in the side, and given him a lesson in fashion. He had marched through locked gates like Superman. That's simply too good to keep to yourself. And why should he?

Obviously, some other folks needed a lesson in "doubt deliverance"! He started with the church folk, those who had failed to practice what they preached. They were doing spiritual things, "many people had gathered and were praying," but when the answer came, they couldn't believe it! "'Peter is at the door!' 'You're out of your mind,' they told her" (vv. 14-15). I've been in some circles like that! And I've learned that all the piety in the world is no substitute for simply accepting the proofs of God's miracles!

"It must be his angel," they tried to explain (v. 15). I can almost read their minds: "Let's put this in sanctified perspective." "Let's not get too excited about something supernatural. We might be labeled as extremists! Let's write our own version of the events."

But these folks weren't the first to look for umbrellas during an outpouring. John the Baptist had his own doubts.

> After Jesus had finished instructing his twelve disciples, he went on from there to teach and preach in the towns of Galilee. When John heard in prison what Christ was doing, he sent his disciples to ask him, "Are you the one who was to come, or should we expect someone else?" Jesus replied, "Go back and report to John what you hear and see: The blind receive sight, the lame walk, those who have leprosy are cured, the deaf hear, the dead are raised, and the good news is preached to the poor. Blessed is the man who does not fall away on account of me" (*Matt. 11:1-6*).

The very One whom John the Baptist had spent most of his ministry telling folks about had arrived, and the fellow with the camel-hair suit was now questioning both the person and the powers of the Christ! Why? His situation wasn't the most hopeful. Every blessing he had prophesied was clouded by the predicament he was in.

Jesus didn't chastise him for his doubt; He simply reminded him that "confession is good for the soul." Confessing God's miracles instead of questioning His presence is a good antidote for overcoming doubt. Telling others about the things God has done for you not only helps others with alleviating their own doubts but also helps you overcome yours!

Jesus said, "Whoever acknowledges me before men, I will also acknowledge him before my Father in heaven" (Matt. 10:32). "I'll tell you, but don't you dare tell anyone else!" Sound familiar? It happens now and then. "Gospel gossip." Sharing "prayer concerns." The positive side of that malady is telling the *good* things that God has done—especially in your own life. That "confession" cuts through clouds of doubt like a butter knife through whipped cream cheese.

Take a look at one last step.

INCREASE YOUR PERSISTENCE LEVEL

Peter had to convince the "convinced" that God had worked a miracle. He had to preach to the choir about overcoming doubts.

> But Peter kept on knocking, and when they opened the door and saw him, they were astonished. Peter motioned with his hand for them to be quiet and described how the Lord had brought him out of prison. "Tell James and the brothers about this," he said, and then he left for another place (*Acts 12:16-17*).

Like a timid Fuller Brush salesperson, Peter could have hit the road after he knocked on the door and didn't get an answer. But he stayed. And he kept knocking. Overcoming doubt takes a "stick-to-it." Jesus taught us about persistence.

> Suppose one of you has a friend, and he goes to him at midnight and says, "Friend, lend me three loaves of bread,

because a friend of mine on a journey has come to me, and I have nothing to set before him." Then the one inside answers, "Don't bother me. The door is already locked, and my children are with me in bed. I can't get up and give you anything." I tell you, though he will not get up and give him the bread because he is his friend, yet because of the man's boldness he will get up and give him as much as he needs. So I say to you: Ask and it will be given to you; seek and you will find; knock and the door will be opened to you. For everyone who asks receives; he who seeks finds; and to him who knocks, the door will be opened (*Luke 11:5-10*).

Overcoming doubt is like a fresh breeze on a hot summer day in Georgia. It inspires and refreshes others. It gives hope in spite of the heat. And it causes others to reach for their own funeral home fans. "In the morning, there was no small commotion among the soldiers as to what had become of Peter" (Acts 12:18).

Let's put those first baby steps on rewind:

1. *Pray.* Prayer is the first line of defense against doubting. It takes you into the presence of God and puts the present circumstances on pause.

2. *Trust.* Don't underestimate the power of God for your predicament.

3. *Obedience.* Do what God says, even if you don't know the what, where, when, and how of your way out.

4. *Thanksgiving.* Begin to praise God for the "answers," even when your head and heart are still full of questions.

5. *Confession.* Openly declare your belief that God is great and God is God.

6. *Persistence.* Never give up!

Get Your Thumb Out of Your Mouth, and Quit Whining—Get a Life!

Overcoming Hopelessness

David's travel itinerary not only took him "beside the still waters" but also "through the valley of the shadow." Throughout the Scriptures, the boy who slew Goliath with a single stone and grew to be king of Israel walked both the peaks and valleys of life, experiencing life's best and worst, feeling despair as well as victory. And at times he was a poster child for hopelessness.

He wasn't the first to take the back alley through the valley of despair, however, and he won't be the last. Whether it's Monday or not, getting the "blues"—experiencing feelings of hopelessness and helplessness—is a common problem. ABC News writer John McKenzie reported a *Journal of the American Medical Association* finding: "About 16 percent of the U.S. adult population will have a major depression at some time in their life. And about as many as 14 million Americans suffered an episode of depression in the last year alone, with the average episode lasting about four months."[1]

In TV talk, for some the episodes of despair turn to a series and then go into reruns. The clouds are as frequent as past episodes of *The Andy Griffith Show*. In Ps. 6 David is singing the blues. Perhaps suffering a medical problem with its accompanying emotional fatigue, along with opposition from his enemies, David is experiencing feelings of rejection and hopelessness. But the solution is right there in the problem. Let's notice the scripture sequence.

DAVID'S SIGHING

After David had taken a long look at what had happened to him—or what was happening at the moment—he realized that his life had been reduced to a super-sized sigh! "O LORD, do not rebuke me in your anger or discipline me in your wrath. Be merciful to me, LORD, for I am faint; O LORD, heal me, for my bones are in agony. My soul is in anguish. How long, O LORD, how long?" (Ps. 6:1-3). The problem is serious. Life, even kingly life, had become a hopeless endeavor. Notice some of the symptoms:

I am faint. David's despair had left him in a weakened state. His spiritual and emotional pulse was so low he would need a visiting antacid salesman to hold him up in the chair of the blood pressure testing machines at the pharmacy! His physical symptoms had chipped away at his emotions until he was ready to point an accusing finger even at the Lord—the very One who had sustained him through so many circumstances in the past. Society has a one-word expression for the feelings of futility he was experiencing: "Whatever."

You don't have to lose your balance on a wobbly throne to know how King David felt.

- A chronic physical condition has taken almost every ounce of your strength.
- You've had to get an additional "In" box for your work desk at the office.
- Family, friends, or coworkers are wearing you down with a to-do list that's taller than you.
- You've had to replace your personal data assistant twice because you ran out of memory in the calendar mode.
- Hopelessness has set in big-time.
- Daily pressures have left you feeling as vibrant as an old dollar bill.
- The power company is whistling "Happy Days Are Here Again" when they send you late payment notices.
- The love of your life left a "Dear John" message on your answering machine.

God's Word has a tiny verse that packs a mighty wallop for emotional feelings like that: "Cast all your anxiety on him because he cares for you" (1 Pet. 5:7).

My bones are in agony. David's feelings of hopelessness had burrowed deep into his psyche and blossomed in physical pain. No doubt the pain was real and may have resulted from a genuine physical ailment. Whatever the source, the king felt about as kingly as an assistant supervisor in the stable-cleaning division of his kingdom.

Pain, whether from a psychological or physiological source, reaches the very core of your being. Your suffering may affect every area of your life: your relationships, your vocation, your self-esteem, your spirituality. And it may seem that all of the world's aspirin wouldn't be enough to relieve the anxiety and discomfort you're feeling.

My soul is in anguish. David's pain reached farther than his bones; it went deep into the spiritual corners of his heart. He felt so out of sorts with himself that he even wondered about his relationship with the Lord. God had chosen him to be king. He had been strengthened with His wisdom. He had heard the melodies and lyrics of heaven's songs in his heart (and had written them down). But now he was in pain, facing the "worst of times" in a "best-case scenario."

DAVID'S CRYING

Sometimes our sighing turns to crying. Tears of hopelessness flow from our trials. It happened to David:

> Turn, O LORD, and deliver me; save me because of your unfailing love. No one remembers you when he is dead. Who praises you from the grave? I am worn out from groaning; all night long I flood my bed with weeping and drench my couch with tears. My eyes grow weak with sorrow; they fail because of all my foes (*Ps. 6:4-7*).

His weeping signaled his loss of hope.

1. David lost hope because he thought God had abandoned him. "Turn, O LORD, and deliver me." David was changing a flat tire in the northbound lane on the freeway of life, and suddenly he thought he saw the Lord traveling southbound—without stopping or even noticing his plight. Maybe David even hit the *OnStar* button in his chariot and no one answered, at least not in his mind. The hopelessness of the moment overshadowed his knowledge of the Almighty.

David forgot that God was mighty enough to travel both directions at once. The northbound travelers wouldn't be ignored while the southbound travelers received His full attention. (And He wouldn't even have to slow down!) David would later write,

> O LORD, you have searched me and you know me. You know when I sit and when I rise; you perceive my thoughts from afar. You discern my going out and my lying down; you are familiar with all my ways. Before a word is on my tongue you know it completely, O LORD. You hem me in —behind and before; you have laid your hand upon me. Such knowledge is too wonderful for me, too lofty for me to attain. Where can I go from your Spirit? Where can I flee from your presence? If I go up to the heavens, you are there; if I make my bed in the depths, you are there. If I rise on the wings of the dawn, if I settle on the far side of the sea, even there your hand will guide me, your right hand will hold me fast (*Ps. 139:1-10*).

2. David lost hope because he lost sight of the eternal. "No one remembers you when he is dead. Who praises you from the grave?" (Ps. 6:5). David thought, *I'm on a slippery slope, slip-sliding toward the family plot in the cemetery near Jerusalem.* Hopelessness focuses on the past and the present. *Memories* of the past or *miseries* of the present are constantly in mind. David even measured his usefulness in terms of his hopelessness: "Who praises you from the grave?"

The king was bowing to the circumstances of time; but the God of eternity was actually in control, moving the chess pieces of David's times toward a final and eternal checkmate and win. "The eternal God is your refuge, and underneath are the everlasting arms" (Deut. 33:27).

3. David lost hope because he equated God's *slow* response with *no* response. "I am worn out from groaning; all night long I flood my bed with weeping and drench my couch with tears" (Ps. 6:6). He had turned his life around, going from weeping and groaning to groaning and weeping! Like the Israelites on their slave march to Babylon, the worship leader had hung his harp of praise on a poplar tree and sang the dirges of earthly despair (Ps. 137).

The microwave generation knows all about the problem. They spend their time, talent, and treasures seeking quick fixes for age-old situations, not realizing that age-old situations have already been fixed. Before the first planet had turned in orbit, the God of the universe had seen David's plight and had a rescue in mind. But God's plans are fulfilled in His time zone. He may not seemingly jump when our first tear falls, but we can be sure that He's on the way. My friend Aaron Wilburn wrote a song titled "Four Days Late," which described the wait between the death of Lazarus and the miracle of Jesus in raising him from the dead (John 11:17-25), saying that even when the Lord is four days late, He's still on time. Groaning and weeping are only temporary. Joy is God's final answer. David finally figured it out: "Weeping may remain for a night, but rejoicing comes in the morning" (Ps. 30:5).

4. David lost hope because he focused on those who were against him rather than one who was for him. "My eyes grow weak with sorrow; they fail because of all my foes" (Ps. 6:7). It was the last set in the tennis tournament of time, and he had just "double-faulted." For those who aren't tennis players, that means he hit his serve into the net twice in a row, giving the point to his opponent. But the match wasn't over! Just because his opponent scored a point, it didn't mean that he or she would win the trophy.

It's the same today. Your opponent (persons or problems) may score a few points, and you may be down "love forty" (0 to 40, in tennis terms), but it's not time to put away the racket. God has the last word on wins and losses. The apostle Paul reminds us:

If God is for us, who can be against us? He who did not spare his own Son, but gave him up for us all—how will he not also, along with him, graciously give us all things? Who will bring any charge against those whom God has chosen? It is God who justifies. Who is he that condemns? Christ Jesus, who died—more than that, who was raised to life—is at the right hand of God and is also interceding for us. Who shall separate us from the love of Christ? Shall trouble or hardship or persecution or famine or nakedness or danger or sword? As it is written: "For your sake we face death all day long; we are considered as sheep to be slaughtered." No, in all these things we are more than conquerors through him who loved us. For I am convinced that neither death nor life, neither angels nor demons, neither the present nor the future, nor any powers, neither height nor depth, nor anything else in all creation, will be able to separate us from the love of God that is in Christ Jesus our Lord (*Rom. 8:31-39*).

David's crying was in vain. God had already granted a victory over his enemies. In other words, the king was sleeping on a soggy sofa for nothing!

David made a winning discovery.

DAVID'S RELIANCE

After a long night of weeping, David finally woke up! The mighty king had to abandon the throne of his life and put the sovereign Lord in his place. It was then that he received help for his hopelessness. David had to admit that God was in control of the situation and that God had the only wise solution:

> Away from me, all you who do evil, for the LORD has heard my weeping. The LORD has heard my cry for mercy; the LORD accepts my prayer. All my enemies will be ashamed and dismayed; they will turn back in sudden disgrace (*Ps. 6:8-10*).

Notice David's steps of faith and reliance.

1. David declared victory. "Away from me, all you who do evil, for the LORD has heard my weeping" (Ps. 6:8). David openly acknowledged that hope was on the way. And the more he said it out loud, the deeper he felt it in his heart. After their setback in not being able to rebuke a demon that had plagued a young boy to whom they were ministering, the disciples went whining to Jesus and said, "How come we couldn't do that like the other disciples?" Jesus said to His disciples, "Because you have so little faith." Ouch! The disciples felt the sting. Then Jesus talked over their heads to all of us who face overwhelming situations with only a cup full of confidence: "I tell you the truth, if you have faith as small as a mustard seed, you can say to this mountain, 'Move from here to there' and it will move. Nothing will be impossible for you" (Matt. 17:20).

Maybe you've noticed a TV close-up of athletes talking to themselves before attempting a game-winning or record-breaking try. What are they saying? I'm not a very good lip-reader, but I assure you that they're *not* saying:

"I can't do this."

"This is hopeless."

"I tried this once before and fell on my nose."

"I'm just going to settle for third place."

"I don't have enough spring in my Nikes to pull this one off!"

No, they're talking victory. They're reminding themselves of their ability to overcome the obstacle in their way. In essence, they're rebuking hopelessness *out loud*! When David declared the beginning of his faith, he was pronouncing a finish to his despair. "The LORD has heard my weeping." He had a spiritual breakthrough! His enemies might as well have torn down their pop-up trailers and put their water pistols back into their holsters. His prayers had reached the throne in faith. Notice: *has heard.* There wasn't a "maybe" in sight. John the apostle described that confidence: "Everyone born of God overcomes the world. This is the victory that has overcome the world, even our faith" (1 John 5:4).

God has more promises *in reserve* than you'll ever use in a lifetime of pain or problems. Read them. Underline them. Memorize them. Sing them. Say them out loud. There's nothing that makes the devil as nervous as when he hears a child of God shouting Scripture promises at him!

2. David reminded God of his status. "The LORD has heard my cry for mercy; the LORD accepts my prayer." That wasn't news to God. He heard David's prayer before it was ever formed in his mind. David was the anointed king who belonged to the King of Kings. He didn't need to remind God of who belonged to whom—he needed to remind *himself.* "I am accepted! I may be going through the most difficult days of my life, but God still belongs to me, and I still belong to Him!"

Relying on God begins with reaffirming your relationship with Him. Old Testament warriors voiced it during their marches into battle. New Testament soldiers declared it in the darkness of their prison dungeons. Saints of old and *saints of new* have reminded God that, no matter what, they belonged to Him—and He belonged to them. The reminder gave them courage to face the unexpected, un-called for, and unexplainable. "God is for us!"

One of the first tricks of the enemy is to convince you that your plight is the result of your fright or flight. "You've *done that*, so now you *deserve this*." Rom. 8:15 says, "You did not receive a spirit that makes you a slave again to fear, but you received the Spirit of sonship. And by him we cry, '*Abba*, Father.'" Through faith in Christ and a complete surrender to God's master plan for your life, you're already a victor. God is your father, and He's not about to stand by with His arms crossed while the bullies of hell beat you up!

Claim your right of inheritance. God's power, purpose, plan, and presence are yours by spiritual birthright. When you remind God of your status, you're speaking words of courage to your heart—and overcoming hopelessness in the process.

3. David declared war. He wasn't going to pronounce the benediction, sing the doxology, and then head for the cafeteria to beat the Nazarenes to the serving line. He flat-out declared war on his problems and persecutors. "All my enemies will be ashamed and dismayed; they will turn back in sudden disgrace" (Ps. 6:10). Suddenly the king with the downcast face was "in the face" of his foes. "Bring it on, boys!"

Sometimes you just have to get tough with the opposition. You need to say, "I refuse to be a victim of this despair! I will take every promise in the Book as my strength, and I will whoop the forces of the enemy with a heart full of faith and a mind full of strength!"

I like the way a poet expressed it:

Doubt sees the obstacles; faith sees the way.

Doubt sees the darkest night; faith sees the day.

Doubt dreads to take a step; faith soars on high.

Doubt questions, "Who believes?"

Faith answers, "I."

—Source unknown

Hopelessness has a conqueror: Jesus Christ. "Let us fix our eyes on Jesus, the author and perfecter of our faith, who for the joy set before him endured the cross, scorning its shame, and sat down at the right hand of the throne of God" (Heb. 12:2). Your faith is a freeway to hope. Get on the entrance ramp. It's the fantastic way out of the valley of the shadow— and a direct route to the mountaintop of joy.

David made the discovery. So may you. There's a sunrise on your horizon, a light at the end of your tunnel, a song for your sorrow. My prayer is that you will make the wonderful discovery this very day.

Two Steps Forward and Three Steps Backward
Overcoming Failure

The New Age movement isn't that new. All the essentials, from crystals to palm reading to psychic predictions, were present in biblical times as well. And one New Testament character named Simon was a star player. Today Simon might be a headliner in Las Vegas. Back then he was a headliner in Samaria. His magic acts and psychic powers drew sellout crowds.

Failure isn't that new either. Ever since there have been report cards, job evaluations, or game-winning jump shots at the buzzer of basketball championships, someone has been on the wrong side of the scoreboard. Adrian Rogers, the great late pastor from Memphis, said on television, "Some say we're born crying, live complaining, and die disappointed." Failure doesn't have a class distinction either. Simon proves it.

As a sports enthusiast, I've read about the "topsy-turvies" of athletics. For example, pro basketball players are said to miss an average of 50 percent of their shots. Professional baseball players consider it a victory if they can get on base 3 out of 10 times at bat. And history records that Babe Ruth, one of the greatest hitters of all time, had an enormously high strikeout average.

Everyone from kings to carpenters has experienced the "Humpty Dumptys," the hurt of falling from high places and not being able to put themselves back together again. Sometimes the "fall from *place*" takes on a rather humorous tone. I heard of a professor of business administration who had applied to several universities without as much as a single response. Finally he received one. The letter said that the professor's application had been received and also explained that his "attached résumé" was being returned because it was actually a receipt from the local instant oil change franchise for the professor's last vehicle service. Oops! His absent-minded action was a self-inflicted wound right to the heart of his career. The poor prof is probably working in a fast-food restaurant right now, contemplating either his next career move, his next oil change, or whether the customer wanted his or her fries super-sized!

Simon had a few slip-ups of his own. Seen briefly in the New Testament Book of Acts, his life exemplifies the rises and falls of many. Not much is known about Simon's background. His last name is Magus (obviously not a stage name!). He lived in an area known as Samaria in an age of spiritual experimentation not unlike our own. In a time when religious folk were doing their own thing, practicing just about everything but the principles of the gospel, Simon was one of their gurus. Relatively unknown to most modern church-goers, Simon briefly rose from the fields of biblical obscurity to teach us about the ups and downs of human failure.

Maybe you've had a few ups and downs yourself. And maybe you're either in the failure mode or recovery mode right now. You may be saying "I like God's sense of humor, but I don't get the joke!" Your life has taken a turn for the worst. If so, then take a look at this biblical character with a zoom lens, and discover some reasons for failure and the hope of recovery.

Failure Often Results from an Unfulfilled Need

My friend and mentor for many years, John Maxwell, often said at our INJOY seminars, "No matter what happens to you, failure is always an inside job." It was for Simon:

> Now for some time a man named Simon had practiced sorcery in the city and amazed all the people of Samaria. He boasted that he was someone great, and all the people, both high and low, gave him their attention and exclaimed, "This man is the divine power known as the Great Power." They followed him because he had amazed them for a long time with his magic (*Acts 8:9-11*).

Simon had some inner needs that resulted in an embarrassing fall from the graces of the crowd.

Simon needed better "I"-sight. "He boasted that he was someone great" (v. 9). Often when someone boasts of popularity or power, he or she is in desperate need of both. This perceived lack of recognition or accomplishment, which may date all the way back to childhood, has created an inner vacuum that only the praises of others will fill. And living on that emotional fault line can lead to a personal earthquake.

Overcoming failure begins at home in your heart. What are you holding there that keeps you from realizing your goals? A poor self-image? Harbored resentment? A misconception of God's approval? You may need to get your "I's" checked. God's already approved of you (Ps. 139)—not necessarily your actions or reactions but *you*.

Simon needed the crowd's approval. Simon started believing his own "bio sheet." And all those *endorsements* turned to *endorphins.* A chemical reaction in his brain dulled his pain and produced excitement instead of enlightenment. One of my favorite blooper stories is of a nervous master of ceremonies who introduced the evening's famous speaker: "Now, folks, let's give our speaker a great big round of *applesauce!*"

That was about the consistency of Simon's audience reaction: Applesauce—syrupy, sweet, but without much substance. These folks were looking for spiritual shortcuts, and without his knowledge they had tagged Simon to be their tour guide. But the fact is that *Simon* needed a tour guide.

Who's measuring your perceived failures? Are you looking at the grandstands, or are you keeping your eyes on the track? Learn a lesson from the world of motor sports. NASCAR's best drivers are those who have the best focus. They keep their eyes on the road. The track is surrounded by thousands of fans who have opinions about the drivers' abilities or actions. Suppose a driver pulled over to the grandstand during a race and asked the crowd, "How's my driving?" That driver wouldn't spend a lot of time in Victory Lane!

Simon needed power. You've probably witnessed a performance by actors who hadn't taken the time to learn their lines. The awkwardness of their mumbling and bumbling probably made the performance more of an endurance than an enjoyment. Simon played the "power" role, but he really didn't know his part: "This man is the divine power known as the Great Power" (v. 10), his audience said. But the first time the rabbit didn't jump out of his hat, Simon would be caught. He was resting on his reputation—and that was a scary situation.

Failure often results from someone playing too big a "part." Pretending they have some supernatural power, they eventually let others down—and let themselves down even farther. Essentially, they set themselves up for a failure by operating too far outside the box, outside their gift or ability zone. You know what you can do, better than anyone else. Overcoming failure may begin with learning to say no.

Simon needed the routine. He took the rut instead of the high road. "They followed him because he had amazed them for a long time with his magic" (v. 11). Simon got stuck in the "same old same old." He figured, "If it ain't broke, don't fix it." He needed the familiar. But he was so afraid of not doing things the same way that he didn't notice that some fixing was in order. Failure is often the result of fear:

- Fear of trying
- Fear of failing
- Fear of the unknown
- Fear of public opinion

Simon's fear didn't have anything to do with being outside his "gifted" zone. He was simply afraid to risk the loss of the crowd. As long as the autograph-seekers were still around, he figured it was best to keep up appearances. It may be the same for you. You may be as uncomfortable as a squirrel in the middle of a freeway, but a giant leap into the unknown—trying on a new "hat"—may be just the thing to give you a shot of "vitamin C" (confidence).

FAILURE ISN'T PERMANENT

One of your greatest successes may come right after one of your most embarrassing failures. You're not locked in to failure. "Though a righteous man falls seven times, he rises again, but the wicked are brought down by calamity" (Prov. 24:16). Your next move may put you over the top. Simon made that discovery in his spiritual life.

Simon had an "Aha!" moment that catapulted him out of the box. Against the backdrop of the "New Age" practices of the people of Samaria, an evangelistic crusade was going on, and the apostle Philip was the evangelist. "But when they believed Philip as he preached the good news of the kingdom of God and the name of Jesus Christ, they were baptized, both men and women" (Acts 8:12).

The gospel always changes things! The good news of a proven solution for everyone's failures was better than a zillion magic shows. The people of Samaria didn't need any more entertainment or spiritual speculations—they needed deliverance from the very core of their problems. They needed a solid solution for sin. And the solution was in the person of the Lord Jesus Christ, who gave himself as a sacrifice for the penalty of everyone's disobedience against the will and Word of God, with all its accompanying spiritual and moral failure.

Simon broke the cycle of false religion. "Simon himself believed and was baptized. And he followed Philip everywhere, astonished by the great signs and miracles he saw" (v. 13). The "Great Power" recognized his powerlessness to deal with the number-one problem: himself. He had about as much purpose in his life as a leaf in a windstorm. More than anything, he needed a railing for the stairway of life, something to hold onto on his way up—after being on his way down.

He saw *real* signs and miracles, and he broke the cycle of spiritual poverty. After a glimpse of the real, the glitter of the fake and fakery was gone. It could be the same for you. You may have spent a lifetime "playing church." Maybe, in your entire life, you've never made the discovery of knowing Christ in a personal way. You need to break the cycle of "religion" and form a spiritual relationship with God through faith in the Lord Jesus Christ.

Simon broke the cycle of depending on self. As it was, Simon was only a step away from the edge of the stage. A couple of bad predictions, a miscue, a failed solution, and he was in for a tumble—and the crowds wouldn't be giving him any more "rounds of *applesauce.*" Someone said that when you pour yourself into yourself, the only thing you get out of it is yourself. That's not much hope for these days of *extreme* expectations! Simon broke the cycle of self-righteousness and self-motivation.

It will always be nerve-racking to feed off your own supply. Every one of us needs spiritual "outsourcing." What you can't do on your own God can do for you and through you. "My God will meet all your needs according to his glorious riches in Christ Jesus" (Phil. 4:19). Break the cycle of self-dependence, and start living a God-dependent life. It's a sure cure for failure!

Simon broke the cycle of following the wrong crowd. He had been part of the crowd that was putting its faith in the human. Occultism was the driving force in the Samaritans' search for faith. New Testament apostle Paul encountered a similar crowd when he was on a layover in Athens during a missionary journey. The time out didn't last long. Paul took a look around and began to do what he did best: preach the gospel.

Paul then stood up in the meeting of the Areopagus and said: "Men of Athens! I see that in every way you are very religious. For as I walked around and looked carefully at your objects of worship, I even found an altar with this inscription: TO AN UNKNOWN GOD. Now what you worship as something unknown I am going to proclaim to you. The God who made the world and everything in it is the Lord of heaven and earth and does not live in temples built by hands. And he is not served by human hands, as if he needed anything, because he himself gives all men life and breath and everything else" (*Acts 17:22-25*).

Simon aligned himself with the crowd who believed in the "Lord of heaven and earth [who] does not live in temples built by hands." That changed everything. He took a giant step from spiritual failure to triumphant faith and broke the cycle of dependence on the crowd.

The nice thing about failure: It doesn't have to be a setback; it can be a step forward. "We are hard pressed on every side, but not crushed; perplexed, but not in despair; persecuted, but not abandoned; struck down, but not destroyed" (2 Cor. 4:8-9). You can rise from where you are to where you want to be (and ought to be). Granted, some who have overcome failure have failed again. But you'll also have to admit that some of the most infamous failures have also risen to an even greater faith. We've already discussed how Jesus' trusted disciple Peter denied the Christ, was forgiven, and then went on to become a pillar of the Church. He blazed the trail for each of us.

FAILURE RESULTS FROM TAKING THE EASY WAY INSTEAD
OF THE RIGHT WAY

Sadly, Simon was sidetracked. He drifted back to the spiritual lowlands, like a rhinoceros to a mud hole. Was it the crowd? Partly. But this time it was also about winning the lottery. He began to focus on the *payoff* instead of the *paid-off.* I'm not here to judge his faith; I'm here to raise an eyebrow at his faithfulness.

The good news of the outpouring of the Holy Spirit came to Samaria through Philip's preaching.

When they arrived, they prayed for them that they might receive the Holy Spirit, because the Holy Spirit had not yet come upon any of them; they had simply been baptized into the name of the Lord Jesus. Then Peter and John placed their hands on them, and they received the Holy Spirit (*Acts 8:15-17*).

The great promise of a "Comforter," who would purify, equip, and energize the Christian, had been fulfilled (John 14:26). Heaven's "power cord" had been connected to the Church. And the whole world would feel the electrical current of Pentecost. "You will receive power when the Holy Spirit comes on you; and you will be my witnesses in Jerusalem, and in all Judea and Samaria, and to the ends of the earth" (Acts 1:8).

Notice: "and Samaria." The very core of a false religion would feel the genuine flames of Pentecostal fire. And Simon was right in the path. The only problem: he was going in the wrong direction.

When Simon saw that the Spirit was given at the laying on of the apostles' hands, he offered them money and said,

"Give me also this ability so that everyone on whom I lay my hands may receive the Holy Spirit" (*Acts 8:18-19*).

Learn from Simon's missteps.

Simon returned to the cycle of self. "Give me." His faith turned as phony as a 30-cent piece, and his purpose turned suddenly selfish. Some might say that his entrepreneurial spirit kicked in, and he saw a franchise in his future. "Power Bars." "Instant Power." "PowerAid." Dollar signs floated in his mind and heart. There was nothing wrong with his spirit of entrepreneurship, but there was everything wrong with the spirit from which it blossomed. Cutting-edge marketing without a consecrated heart would only lead him back into the rut of spiritual failure. Jesus warned, "No servant can serve two masters. Either he will hate the one and love the other, or he will be devoted to the one and despise the other. You cannot serve both God and Money" (Luke 16:13).

You will always be tempted to rely more on yourself than on God. That tendency goes all the way back to the Garden of Eden (Gen. 3). Refuse to make the U-turn. God's path may have a few construction zones along the way, but it will always get you to the right place. "As for God, his way is perfect; the word of the LORD is flawless. He is a shield for all who take refuge in him" (Ps. 18:30).

Simon returned to the wrong crowd. He had broken the cycle of needing their affirmation by aligning himself with Philip's converts. Now he was looking back to his former cronies. He assumed that with some store-bought spiritual power he could resume his role as a guru to the Samaritans. It was "fast-food faith," a shortcut around the demands of the gospel and straight to center stage.

Simon's actions put a face on the warning of the wisdom writer: "There is a way that seems right to a man, but in the end it leads to death" (Prov. 14:12). "Work smarter." "Eliminate the middle man." "Fast-track it." "Plan to win." You've heard the world's advice. Actually, there's nothing wrong with the principles as long as they fit in with a Christ-filled, Spirit-led faith. The "easy way out" sometimes leads folks to a back alley rather than the expressway.

In case you're wondering, Simon didn't make it to faith's Hall of Fame. Like an Olympic skater who gave up, he untied his skates before his final routine. The guru of Samaria dropped from the pages of the Book almost as fast as he appeared. But on his way down he pointed us to an important step in overcoming failure. What is it? Repentance.

FAILURE CAN BE THE BEGINNING

Simon entered a gut-wrenching conversation with a key disciple of Christ. He had handed the disciple his Visa card and was about ready to take possession on enough ability to turn the heads of the old crowd. "Peter answered: 'May your money perish with you, because you thought you could buy the gift of God with money! You have no part or share in this ministry, because your heart is not right before God'" (Acts 8:20-21).

Suddenly the "Las Vegas headliner" from Samaria was in the hot seat. The lights from a network news camera crew were shining on him, and he was about as comfortable as a pickpocket at a police convention. But the advice that followed is a great map for traveling out of the wilderness of failure to the road of spiritual victory.

First, acknowledge your failure. The advice to Simon: "Repent of this wickedness and pray to the Lord. Perhaps he will forgive you for having such a thought in your heart" (v. 22). Whether your setbacks have been the result of your disobedience or disregard of God's Word, acknowledge them. Repent of them, that is, be sorry enough to turn from the wrong way to the right.

Second, deal with personal issues that feed failure. Christ's disciple gave Simon a spiritual CAT scan: "For I see that you are full of bitterness and captive to sin" (v. 23). It seems that spiritual CAT scans were prevalent even in Old Testament times. The psalmist David asked for one: "Search me, O God, and know my heart; test me and know my anxious thoughts" (Ps. 139:23).

The Holy Spirit is faithful to reveal the deepest needs of your heart. Don't be afraid of His searching. And once He brings those inner needs to the surface, give them to Him. Confess them. Trust His forgiveness. And claim victory over them. I've spoken in 48 of the United States and two continents, with only a few incidents. Once I was touring a city when a college student who had borrowed her mother's SUV accidentally rear-ended my friend Wayne Brewer's car. I was in the back seat minding my own business. Funny how that gets your attention! All at once your head changes directions. You're going in one direction, and suddenly your brain hits the skids!

My friend Wayne and I went to console the young lady, who was probably thinking not only about wrecking her mother's car but also about the sudden depletion in her college funds. We assured her that her mother would be more concerned about her than the SUV. We were right. A cell phone call brought the mother to the scene. The first words out of her mouth were, "Are you all right?" The next action was an embrace. Forgiveness won out over faulty driving. If that can happen on the highway, it can happen in your spiritual life as well. When you trust God for forgiveness, He'll come to the scene with an embrace.

Third, acknowledge your dependence upon God. Once again, Simon was reminded of his weakness—and God's strength. Notice his response: "Pray to the Lord for me so that nothing you have said may happen to me" (Acts 8:24). The enemy of your faith doesn't have to write "Finish" across the chapters of your life. Just because he's a loser, it doesn't mean you have to be one. You can make the most important transfer of your life—turning your life completely over to God. You can put your trust in the One who can be trusted when everyone and everything else fails you: Christ.

Failure can be a beginning. You can start from here—even if you have to start over. You can reach the finish line without being *finished!* I like the way this philosopher put it:

Failure is not failing to reach your dreams:
Failure is not having a dream. Failure is not setting
a goal and missing it: Failure is not having a goal.

Failure is not falling down: Failure is refusing to
get back up *(source unknown)*.

No Matter Where You Go, There You Are

Overcoming Loneliness

Three guys were stranded on an island. One day a bottle washed up on the shore. When they popped the cork, a genie appeared. Each man was granted one wish in return for freeing the genie. The first man said, "I miss my family in Phoenix. I wish to return to them." He was gone in a flash. The second was so excited after seeing his friend disappear that he shouted, "I'm from New York and I want to go home!" Zap! He was gone, and the third man stood all alone on the island and moaned about not having anyplace to go.

The genie insisted that the third man make a wish, otherwise it would be confined to its bottle once again. The guy thought for a few moments and then said, "Oh, all right. I wish those two guys were back here!"[1]

The fact is you don't have to be on an island to feel loneliness. You can be in the heart of the largest city in the world and still feel as if you're "home alone." Counselors tell us that loneliness is one of the greatest problems in our society. So in one sense, we're not alone when we feel lonely.

In a greater sense, we really aren't alone when we feel lonely. The God who put us together knows what makes us tick. He saw our lonely days even before the world was formed—and He planned to do something about them. They come as no surprise to Him, even when they surprise us.

Not long ago, I was driving my wife's car (which she lets me do when it needs gas or a wash) and listening to the "oldies" station on the radio. Elvis was singing one of his greatest hits, and the lyric struck me, about taking a walk down "Lonely Street" to "Heartbreak Hotel." I have friends who knew the great entertainer, and they say that feelings of loneliness plagued Elvis Presley throughout his life. He was familiar with those walks down lonely streets.

That route may be familiar to you as well. If so, I'm glad to be able to share some principles that you may use to overcome loneliness. We might identify five words that define loneliness:

Detachment

Separation

Desolation

Solitude

Isolation

Each of those words could be used to describe an incident in the life of Jesus. The writer to the Hebrews said, "For we do not have a high priest who is unable to sympathize with our weaknesses, but we have one who has been tempted in every way, just as we are—yet was without sin" (Heb. 4:15). Jesus not only experienced loneliness—He conquered it, along with everything else that plagues the human spirit. His Word is a trusted tour guide down the lonely streets.

Notice several important observations about loneliness.

LONELINESS IS COMMON

When I recently "Googled" the word "loneliness" on the Internet, the result proved how common the problem really is: my search brought up over two million pages. Two million web pages filled with definitions, treatments, support groups, books, tapes, and programs devoted to loneliness! Unbelievable. We're living in a world of more than six billion people, and we haven't progressed socially any farther than the Old Testament psalmist who said, "I lie awake; I have become like a bird alone on a roof" (Ps. 102:7).

We have more clubs, more parties, more opportunities for sports and recreation, and more toys than anyone in history, but we're still alone and lonely. Hundreds of years ago the wisdom writer accurately described us:

> There was a man all alone; he had neither son nor brother. There was no end to his toil, yet his eyes were not content with his wealth. "For whom am I toiling," he asked, "and why am I depriving myself of enjoyment?" This too is meaningless—a miserable business! (*Eccles. 4:8*).

Why is loneliness so common?

We're more isolated. The threats and attacks of our times have driven us indoors. We close ourselves behind locked doors and look at fellow humans through security cameras. We type messages to each other on handheld computers or cell phones. We're more content to talk online than in person.

We're more skeptical. We don't talk to strangers. We doubt the word of those we once trusted and believe the word of those we don't really know. And the difference has divided us, put walls of loneliness between us. We live in "red" or "blue" states and thumb our political, social, or religious noses at those who live in the other.

We're more mobile. We don't live in the same houses as long. We move. We're not loyal to a city, town, or neighborhood. We migrate to new areas without considering that we'll be looking for new friends—and sometimes we don't even care. We rent high-rise apartments or low-mortgage-rate houses and live for months or years without knowing either the first or the last name of our nearest neighbor.

We're more technical. We have new friends: electronic games, robotic dogs, iPods, plasma TVs, MP3 players, or TiVos. We're content to be alone with our gizmos, only venturing out to yard sales, where we buy more stuff from people we don't know and bring it back to our family fortresses like squirrels gathering acorns.

We're more secular. Our church used to be the headquarters for our friendships. There, during its services, we spent time with our family and friends three or more times each week. But in many cases, a couple of the weekly services have been dropped from the church calendar. Alternate services (or no services) free us to spend more time with ourselves and less time with our church family. Now we're more familiar with what's going on in sports, politics, or entertainment than we are with what's going on in the church. We watch DVDs. We sit in box seats at baseball or football games—away from the bleacher section. We're alone in the crowd.

We're more active. We often have more than one job (to pay off credit card purchases or to make installment payments on jet skis). We're consumed with being a consumer, so we have to spend more time at work and less time with our friends or family. We "need" the overtime pay and forget that the real payoff will be more stress and less time for those with whom we should spend *more* time.

Loneliness Has a Wide Impact

Jesus' own life patterns the far-reaching effects of loneliness. During His 30-some years on earth, the Son of God experienced both the positive and negative effects of being alone—and lonely.

On the positive side, Jesus used His "alone time" for spiritual refreshment. During His earthly ministry, crowds followed Him everywhere. Seeking His teaching or His healing, the crowd was constantly demanding Him. One incident shows us how the Master used "lonely" times for His own benefit. "After he had dismissed them, he went up on a mountainside by himself to pray. When evening came, he was there alone" (Matt. 14:23).

It was Jesus' favorite time. Alone, away from the crowds, He would spend time with His Heavenly Father in prayer. Quiet times. Alone times. Times that each of us would better ourselves by having.

We have become so busy *doing* that we often neglect *being*. Our souls need a break from our bodies! With all our workouts at the gym, shopping at health food stores, or even getting "tucked away" at the plastic surgeon's clinic, we've been more than gracious to our bodies. But our souls are crying out to us, "Give me some time!"

Lonely times are "soul times." They're reading times. Praying times. Meditating times. Thinking times. Times to strengthen the inner person. Bonding times with our Lord.

Jesus also experienced the downside of loneliness. No one understands like Jesus. That's especially true when it comes to feelings of loneliness.

1. JESUS EXPERIENCED SPIRITUAL LONELINESS.

Christ began His earthly ministry with one of the most intense (and lonely) incidents in His life. Following the baptism that announced heaven's approval of God's only Son (Luke 3:21-22), Jesus had a lonely wilderness experience in which He faced the temptations of the devil. Dr. Luke, the physician-disciple, tells us about it:

> Jesus, full of the Holy Spirit, returned from the Jordan and was led by the Spirit in the desert, where for forty days he was tempted by the devil. He ate nothing during those days, and at the end of them he was hungry.
>
> The devil said to him, "If you are the Son of God, tell this stone to become bread." Jesus answered, "It is written: 'Man does not live on bread alone.'"
>
> The devil led him up to a high place and showed him in an instant all the kingdoms of the world. And he said to him, "I will give you all their authority and splendor, for it has been given to me, and I can give it to anyone I want to. So if you worship me, it will all be yours." Jesus answered, "It is written: 'Worship the Lord your God and serve him only.'"
>
> The devil led him to Jerusalem and had him stand on the highest point of the temple. "If you are the Son of

God," he said, "throw yourself down from here. For it is written: 'He will command his angels concerning you to guard you carefully; they will lift you up in their hands, so that you will not strike your foot against a stone.'" Jesus answered, "It says: 'Do not put the Lord your God to the test.'"

When the devil had finished all this tempting, he left him until an opportune time (*Luke 4:1-13*).

Every child of God can identify with spiritual loneliness. Often after a spiritual victory comes a terrible trek through the lonely wilderness. The crowds are gone. The record book has been closed and stored on a shelf. Another newspaper headline has replaced the one that had your picture under it. And you're alone. The "lord of loneliness" (the devil) comes to you in the eerie quietness and stakes his claims on your spirit.

"You don't need anyone but me and mine. Serve me."

"I can give you everything you ever dreamed of, if you'll just abandon your godly allegiance."

"You don't have to live in the spiritual safety zone. Join the crowd, and have some fun for a change."

Perhaps you've heard his evil whispers. No one else heard them. You were alone and feeling alone. Perhaps you were even searching for a quick fix for your loneliness. The lonely spiritual battle waged, and not even your best friends knew about your inner struggle. Maybe not—but Jesus did. He's already traveled the roads of your wilderness. He's already faced the enemy of your faith. And He won't stand in the street while the enemy is camped on your doorstep. Heb. 13:5 says, "Keep your lives free from the love of money and be content with what you have, because God has said, 'Never will I leave you; never will I forsake you.'" As they say in Oklahoma, "Never? Now that's a good while!"

2. JESUS EXPERIENCED THE LONELINESS OF LEADERSHIP.

Jesus' victory over the devil in the wilderness was only chapter one. There would be other struggles, including the misunderstanding of His closest associates. They misunderstood His talk about a "kingdom," thinking it was a political kingdom that would be established on earth. They even misunderstood the sole purpose of His ministry: His coming to earth to give His life as a sacrifice for sin.

The scene is familiar. We refer to it as "the Last Supper." Jesus the leader was trying to explain His mission to His followers:

> On the first day of the Feast of Unleavened Bread, when it was customary to sacrifice the Passover lamb, Jesus' disciples asked him, "Where do you want us to go and make preparations for you to eat the Passover?" So he sent two of his disciples, telling them, "Go into the city, and a man carrying a jar of water will meet you. Follow him. Say to the owner of the house he enters, 'The Teacher asks: Where is my guest room, where I may eat the Passover with my disciples?' He will show you a large upper room, furnished and ready. Make preparations for us there." The disciples left, went into the city and found things just as Jesus had told them. So they prepared the Passover.
>
> When evening came, Jesus arrived with the Twelve. While they were reclining at the table eating, he said, "I tell you the truth, one of you will betray me—one who

is eating with me." They were saddened, and one by one they said to him, "Surely not I?" "It is one of the Twelve," he replied, "one who dips bread into the bowl with me. The Son of Man will go just as it is written about him. But woe to that man who betrays the Son of Man! It would be better for him if he had not been born."

While they were eating, Jesus took bread, gave thanks and broke it, and gave it to his disciples, saying, "Take it; this is my body." Then he took the cup, gave thanks and offered it to them, and they all drank from it. "This is my blood of the covenant, which is poured out for many," he said to them. "I tell you the truth, I will not drink again of the fruit of the vine until that day when I drink it anew in the kingdom of God." When they had sung a hymn, they went out to the Mount of Olives.

"You will all fall away," Jesus told them, "for it is written: 'I will strike the shepherd, and the sheep will be scattered.' But after I have risen, I will go ahead of you into Galilee." Peter declared, "Even if all fall away, I will not." "I tell you the truth," Jesus answered, "today—yes, tonight—before the rooster crows twice you yourself will disown me three times." But Peter insisted emphatically, "Even if I have to die with you, I will never disown you." And all the others said the same (*Mark 14:12-31*).

Have you ever experienced the loneliness of leadership? I have. My plans and programs have been as misunderstood as a *New York Times* crossword puzzle written in hieroglyphics. Some of my associates have pledged their allegiance and then left. I've had leadership dreams that have become targets for the fiery darts of my enemies. I've felt as if each of my suits had an invisible bull's-eye on the back—especially when I wore it to a business meeting! I'm glad that Jesus understood. I'm glad that no matter where I've been on the corporate or Kingdom ladder, I haven't ascended or descended alone.

You have that same assurance. You're not alone in your leadership—even if you feel lonely. By faith in Christ, you have a "silent partner," one who will bankroll your spiritual leadership investments with His presence, power, and heavenly resources.

You don't have to worry about not having an "uncle in the furniture business"—you have a Brother in the livestock and real estate business—who also collects diamonds! He owns the cattle on a thousand hills and the wealth in every mine (a paraphrase of a song I used to sing in Sunday School).

3. JESUS EXPERIENCED THE LONELINESS OF BETRAYAL.

Have you ever been betrayed by someone you trusted? Jesus was. His own disciple turned on him. It was during the well-known incident in the Garden of Gethsemane. Jesus had gone there to pray, to offer His life up to His Heavenly Father as the offering for every person's sin. He was alone, deep into the garden, in agony, sweating actual drops of blood. His disciples were at the edge of the garden asleep—not a very good security team!

During the "debriefing session" with His disciples, another disciple appeared, accompanied by Roman soldiers. Luke writes, "While he was still speaking a crowd came up, and the man who was called Judas, one of the Twelve, was leading them. He approached Jesus to kiss him, but Jesus asked him, 'Judas, are you betraying the Son of Man with a kiss?'" (Luke 22:47-48). You know the answer as well as Judas did. Jesus received the kiss of betrayal by one of His own. It was the first step on the road to Calvary.

The loneliness of betrayal hovers over the spirit like a London fog. Disbelief clouds the mind. Hurt haunts the soul. If it's happened to you, then you'll be assured to know that there's one who understands. Jesus has felt the hurt of your hurts.

> Since the children have flesh and blood, he too shared in their humanity so that by his death he might destroy him who holds the power of death—that is, the devil—and free those who all their lives were held in slavery by their fear of death. For surely it is not angels he helps, but Abraham's descendants. For this reason he had to be made like his brothers in every way, in order that he might become a merciful and faithful high priest in service to God, and that he might make atonement for the sins of the people. Because he himself suffered when he was tempted, he is able to help those who are being tempted" *(Heb. 2:14-18).*

4. JESUS EXPERIENCED THE LONELINESS OF SEPARATION.

One of the most chilling verses in the Bible is this: "About the ninth hour Jesus cried out in a loud voice, *'Eloi, Eloi, lama sabachthani?'*—which means, 'My God, my God, why have you forsaken me?'" (Matt. 27:46). The God "[whose] eyes are too pure to look on evil" (Hab. 1:13) had to turn away from His only Son, who had taken all the sins of the world on His shoulders. The passion of the Christ not only included the mind-boggling beatings and tormenting of Calvary—it also included the heart-wrenching loneliness of being separated from His Father.

The loneliness of separation can be explained only by one who has suffered it the most: a widowed spouse, grieving parents, an abandoned friend or lover. These are the Purple Heart veterans of separation. They can still feel the loneliness, even after the years have passed.

But these are the ones for whom Christ experienced *the* separation. The very people whose pain reached the very heart of the man on the middle cross. He knows separation as no other. We have God in our times of crisis. He didn't. Though He was God in the flesh, He laid aside the rank and power of God to become like one of us—to suffer our sufferings, to feel more alone in one moment than we would ever feel in a lifetime, to be abandoned by His loving Heavenly Father.

LONELINESS CAN BE OVERCOME

I can't offer you an instant cure for something that maybe has plagued you throughout your life. But I can offer you some solid steps that have been tested in the times of literally thousands of people whom I've been privileged to pastor.

1. Identify your feelings of loneliness. Don't "hide it under a bushel" like a shining little light. Bring it to the surface. Dare to speak like the psalmist, "Turn to me and be gracious to me, for I am lonely and afflicted" (Ps. 25:16). Be honest with yourself about the gray cloud that clings to you even in a crowd.

2. Confess your feelings of loneliness. Be honest with God about your loneliness. Some of those feelings may have resulted from acts of disobedience against His will or His Word. The apostle Paul gave an interesting and Spirit-anointed insight in his letter to Christians: "Once you were alienated from God and were enemies in your minds because of your evil behavior" (Col. 1:21). Some feelings of loneliness are actually feelings of guilt. And guilt is a good candidate for *grace*.

3. Share your feelings of loneliness. Enlist the help of a trusted friend. Two or three dollars for a double latte at the corner coffee shop may be worth the investment. Even if you only have enough money left to get yourself a glass of water, the time you'll spend "downloading" will be time well spent. "God sets the lonely in families, he leads forth the prisoners with singing; but the rebellious live in a sun-scorched land" (Ps. 68:6). You may be an orphaned only child, but through faith in Christ, you have more cousins than you could ever count. Take some of your lonely feelings to a "family reunion"—even if just one of your "family members" shows up.

4. Determine to overcome your feelings of loneliness. You can camp under either of two tents: *con*tent or *dis*content. The *dis*content will always leak in a thunderstorm. When you're under the *con*tent, you'll never notice it! According to Paul, it's a learning process. "I am not saying this because I am in need, for I have learned to be content whatever the circumstances" (Phil. 4:11). Identify your feelings—step one. Decide to do what you can do to break the cycle of loneliness.

5. Overcome your feelings of loneliness by helping someone overcome his or hers. "Carry each other's burdens, and in this way you will fulfill the law of Christ" (Gal. 6:2). Form a support group: you and one other person. And then spend some top-quality "anti-loneliness" time with him or her. Of course, discretion should be used in choosing your support "group" member. Forming close friendships with someone of the opposite sex, especially someone other than a spouse, could lead to other, more severe, problems.

You don't even have to spend time in counseling another. For example, your feelings of loneliness may take flight by helping someone with a landscaping project. Digging up weeds is better than growing those feelings that have caused you emotional pain.

6. Overcome your feelings of loneliness by giving them to God. The words of Jesus bear repeating: "Come to me, all you who are weary and burdened, and I will give you rest. Take my yoke upon you and learn from me, for I am gentle and humble in heart, and you will find rest for your souls" (Matt. 11:28-29). Only in Christ can picking up a yoke of faith result in a lighter load! "Come." "Learn." "Rest." The destination is worth the trip.

In March 2005 the citizens of America were mesmerized by the actions that took place in an Atlanta courthouse. On his way to a court to answer charges of a horrible crime, a young man from a good home overcame a security guard, took the guard's weapon, and went on a killing spree. The judge, a court reporter, and a sheriff's deputy were the first to die.

Reports of the hunt for the killer crawled across television screens, and "special alerts" interrupted programming. But the killing spree came to an awesome ending. The accused wasn't flushed out of a hiding place. There was no gunfire. He gave himself up by waving a white T-shirt or towel from the apartment of a woman he had taken captive hours before.

The woman, Ashley Smith, had accomplished what hundreds of armed police personnel could not do. She convinced him to surrender. Her conversations with the killer throughout the harrowed night had convinced him that she could be trusted.

She was then free to talk to him of her past, with its problems and pain; to talk of her faith, with its failures and gains; to talk about a future, by sharing her purpose in life—and the purpose God had for his life.

Calm, confident, and caring, the captive calmed the killer and brought an end to the fear that had held a major metropolitan city hostage. The biggest obstacle of her life had been overcome—not by might but by faith.

I don't know what holds you captive. I simply know that what seems to be the end could very well be a glorious beginning. You may not have what it takes to be an overcomer, but God does. His help is as big as His heart. And His hand is stronger than your hindrance.

He conquered the grave. He can conquer the very things you thought had conquered you.

Notes

Chapter 3

1. <http://en.thinkexist.com/quotation/all_of_us_are_born_with_a_set_of_instinctive/155885.html>.

2. *Merriam-Webster's Collegiate Dictionary,* 10th ed., s.v. "fear."

3. "Famous and Not So Famous Fear Quotes," <http://www.phobialist.com/fears.html>.

Chapter 5

1. Daniel G. Bagby, *Understanding Anger in the Church* (Nashville: Broadman Press, 1979), 149.

Chapter 6

1. Quoted in Kent and Barbara Hughes, *Liberating Ministry from the Success Syndrome* (Carol Stream, Ill.: Tyndale House Publishers, 1988), 134.

Chapter 8

1. John McKenzie, "More Men Suffer Depression than Seek Help," ABC News, February 12, 2005. Online at <http://abcnews.go.com/WNT/story?id=129631&page=1>.

Chapter 10

1. Jeffrey Johnson, "Overcoming Loneliness, *Reminisce Extra,* August 1994, 60.